SIMPLIFYING YOUR LIFE

Divine Insights to Uncomplicated Living

SIMPLIFYING YOUR LIFE

Divine Insights to Uncomplicated Living

MAC HAMMOND

CONTENTS

INTRODUCTION

There is no question about it. We are living in fast-paced, complex times. Christians and non-Christians alike are facing heavier workloads, greater demands, and higher stress levels than ever before. Not a week goes by that I don't talk to some harried, frazzled believer who laments his inability to spend more time in the Word or get more involved in church because his schedule doesn't permit it.

Most Christians who are living this way know, deep down inside, that something isn't right. They know that something must change. They sense that living this way in the twenty-first century is costing them something—they're just not sure what and how much.

The hard truth is, having an overly complex life will cost you more than you can imagine. But the good news is that there's a way out that doesn't involve winning a lottery or dropping out of society. God has a plan for successfully managing life's resources.

Every person on earth has been entrusted by God with three resources—time, money, and relationships. And if you are to fulfill God's wonderful plan for your life, these three resources must be properly managed. Furthermore, it is the mismanagement of these resources that makes life so complicated.

Think about it for a moment. Mismanage the resource of money and your life can become very complicated, very quickly. Bill collectors, late charges, credit card debt, along with the stress and worry that accompany these things, is a prescription for complexity.

Manage the resource of time poorly, and once again, your life becomes unnecessarily complex.

And nothing else in the world can complicate your life more completely than being a poor manager of relationships. (Ask anyone who has been unfaithful to a spouse how complicated life got as soon as he or she started violating God's law of fidelity.)

Yes, it's nothing more than being a poor manager of the three resources with which we've all been entrusted that is making our lives more complicated. If the goal is a simpler life (and it should be), then we have to become better stewards of these resources.

Are you ready to find out how you can minimize the distractions in your life and maximize the resources you do have? Would you like to learn how to be an effective manager of your time, money, and relationships so that you can focus on the most important things in your life?

Well, I'm about to share some very practical keys to making that happen in each of these three vital areas of your life. But first, we must lay the spiritual foundation.

I invite you to read on and discover God's secrets of *Simplifying Your Life.*

MAKE IT SIMPLE

I've seen it over and over again. The light of God's Word penetrates a person's heart, and positive change happens. Freedom comes. Life comes. I never cease to marvel at the transformational power of the Word.

Yet far too few believers are experiencing those kinds of breakthroughs. And I believe I know why.

The primary reason people don't receive the light that would open them up to a better understanding of God is that life is simply too complex. More people don't enjoy God's presence, God's anointing, or God's glorious plan because life is just too complicated.

Furthermore, there are many people who sit in church or fellowship with other Christians and talk about the Word and the Lord, but they never gain any insight. These people hear the Word, but the *revelation* of the Word never comes. They don't seem to have the ability to absorb the fullness of God's wisdom.

What is the answer? Is life here at the beginning of the twenty-first century so unavoidably complex that nothing can be done short of moving to the mountains and becoming a hermit?

Or is it possible that God's Word holds the very wisdom we can apply that will make our lives simpler, less stressful, and more fertile soil for the transforming power of God? I believe it does.

Is simplifying our lives really the key? Let's see what Psalms 119 has to say about it:

> *The entrance of thy words giveth light; it giveth understanding unto the simple.*
>
> Psalms 119:130

The first part of that verse clearly states, "The entrance of thy words giveth light." This phrase suggests that when somebody sits under the preaching of the Word, light should come. God's revelation should come. But the balance of that verse tells us why this doesn't happen for many people: "It giveth understanding unto the simple."

In our modern vernacular, when we characterize someone as being simple, we are suggesting that he or she has a lower-than-average intellectual capacity. Today if you call somebody simple, he or she will probably take offense. Actually, that's not the only definition of the word *simple* in King James English. One of the Hebrew root words translated *simple* means "open-minded, believing every word (naïve)."[1] So, basically, I see that this verse could read that the Word gives understanding to the open-minded and the uncomplicated.

The entrance of God's Word gives light to those who are open-minded, to those who have simplified their lives. It shows us how He wants us to live our lives and the principles

2

that should govern us. That wisdom, that light, and that understanding come only to the simple.

Complexity in itself doesn't have to be a bad thing. The human body, for example, is a wonderfully complex creation. And there are certain machines man has made that are very complex. These things in themselves aren't bad.

I'm talking about the mismanagement of life's affairs that results in a degree of complexity which makes it difficult to receive the light of God. The reason people don't know God the way they should is that the affairs of their lives have become too complicated.

And if our lives become too complicated, we will never have the understanding necessary to enable us to succeed and overcome life's challenges without some simplification in our lives.

Now, the Bible is a book of answers. And Jesus came to demonstrate those answers and introduce us to the person of God. But if our lives are too complicated, too busy, and filled with too many things that aren't needful, we'll not benefit from the full light and understanding the Bible would bring.

Put another way, if we don't somehow simplify our lives, we'll walk in the darkness of complications. Things won't change very much for us.

Of course, if you're a Christian, you're never in total darkness. According to Colossians 1:13, when you make Jesus your Lord, you're translated from the kingdom of darkness into the kingdom of light. But I'll tell you one thing, many Christians I know are walking in some pretty deep shadows. Why? Because they're not benefiting from the light God has provided for them. They're not walking in the understanding necessary to govern their decisions and illuminate their path. Their lives are too complicated, and as a result, they're walking in the shadows.

Have you ever thought about what it takes to make a shadow? A shadow occurs when something comes between you and the source of light. If that obstruction is large enough, it can cover you with a shadow. That's really a picture of what complications do. They are obstructions that come between you and the light available to you as a Christian.

Complications cast shadows. Therefore, when our lives are too complicated, we can't walk in the benefit of God's light. Understanding doesn't come. So we stumble through life as we would if we were walking in darkness, and we wonder why things don't work the way they should.

For example, we might say, "I don't understand why I'm sick rather than healed," or "I've given my tithes, but I'm still experiencing financial difficulty. I don't understand."

Now, it's true that there are some things the Bible says we're not going to understand until we go home to be with the Lord. We see as through a glass darkly now. (1 Corinthians 13:12) Furthermore, if we could understand everything, we wouldn't need faith. Nevertheless, we *are* supposed to have enough understanding to succeed and prosper. The light of God's Word is sufficient to enable us to overcome. But that light can come only when we simplify our lives. Complications will keep us from receiving the light of God's Word—the light

4

that will illuminate our situation and show us the answer to our problem.

I want to emphasize that complications keep us from receiving the light and understanding we must gain to fulfill God's will for our lives and experience His blessing. So, we *must* simplify our stressed-out, overly complex lives.

GETTING TO KNOW GOD

I'll never forget the day I had a revelation of this subject in my own life. I was elk hunting in the mountains of Colorado just before dawn one gorgeous October morning. It was a special morning. Before me lay a small meadow surrounded by woods that flanked the side of a mountain. I was so captured by the beauty of this scene that I paused for a while to take it all in.

I sat in that meadow very quietly. It's amazing how still the air can get in the mountains. I thought I would at least hear a bird chirping or the wind rushing through the trees, but not that morning. It was so still, I imagined I could hear a pine needle drop from a nearby tree.

It was just starting to get light, and at that moment, the presence of God came upon me so strongly that it's impossible to describe exactly how wonderful it felt. It was as if the golden glow of the morning's first rays had filled my heart with God's beauty and majesty right there in that meadow. The presence of God totally enfolded me. I felt such incredible peace.

And, even as I was experiencing this overwhelming presence of the Lord, a question rose up within my heart. I thought to myself, *God, why do I have to wait until I am in the woods on the side of a mountain for this to happen? Why can't I have this touch from You in other places and during other times in my life?*

Yes, it's true, I've experienced God's presence and His anointing in other ways in moderate degrees. But out there it happened so overwhelmingly that it was hard to believe. And yet while I was sitting there enjoying the experience, pondering my question to God, I thought, *I want this to be something that's a typical part of my life.*

I had a little pocket New Testament and Psalms with me, and soon there was enough light to read, so I pulled it out and began flipping through the Psalms. When I came to Psalms 46:10, I stopped and began reading. Almost as if it was the answer to my unasked question, I read, "Be still and know that I am God."

Right away I knew God was speaking to me. It was so still, and I had never before experienced that kind of stillness and beauty. God was telling me, *Be still and know that I am God.*

In that moment this book was born. Out in the middle of a Colorado meadow at dawn, God gave me the revelation that I'm about to share with you.

KNOW THAT HE IS GOD

The Bible encourages us to *know* that He is God. And we can see, according to Psalms 46:10, that becoming still is an important key to knowing Him. In fact, it is very clear that if we don't fulfill the prerequisite of finding a place of stillness, the implication is, we won't know God.

In other words, we won't know Him as our God unless we're able to achieve something called "a place of stillness." First is being still, next is knowing God. It's the only way we can know God. And I don't think there's anything more important than for a person to know Him.

Let me tell you something. Most Christians know something *about* God, but they don't really *know* God. You see, Christians don't have to be still to know *about* God. One's life doesn't have to be uncomplicated to know *about* God. For example, some Christians may have heard things concerning God's nature, or they may have read something about His acts upon the earth. Some may have even studied about Him in depth, giving them a detailed knowledge about God, but that doesn't mean they necessarily know God.

The only way we can truly know God personally, intimately, is to be still before Him. Likewise, the only way the light of His presence will shine into our lives is to come to a place called stillness.

Knowing God can eliminate problems with distrust or unbelief. For example, we must know God before we can truly have faith.

Let me ask you something: How can you have faith in somebody you don't even know? Obviously, you can't. And yet, faith is what makes all things possible. The Bible says we're to have faith in God. So, we must know God before we can have faith in Him. Once we come to a knowledge of God's faithfulness and integrity, trust and faith come easily.

Not knowing God is the main faith problem in the Church today. People are not speaking with faith when you hear them say, "Well, I'm trying to believe God for my healing. I'm trying to believe that He is meeting my need." These same people don't even know who the "He" is behind the healing or the answer to prayer.

On the other hand, if we know God, we can believe for answers, because we know what His stated will is for our lives, so it's a settled issue. We know He's dependable, generous, and full of goodness. We know He will do what He's promised to do.

You can see how important faith is; by faith, our needs are met. The Bible says, "All things are possible to him that believeth" (Mark 9:23). We can't know God—let alone have faith to believe Him—until we learn to be still.

Knowing God changes our patterns of thinking from legalistic thoughts into thoughts filled with hope, excitement, and exhilaration, because we now have a vital relationship with the Creator of the universe.

Knowing God can turn oppression and heaviness into joy and victory. It's hard to be sad when you know God. God is the source of all peace, joy, and everything good. And when we truly know Him, sadness and depression can't remain in our lives for long!

The secret to a successful walk with God, a fulfilled life in God, a vital Christianity, is in knowing God. That's the definition of a full life. And we find that full life by being still and knowing God.

FINDING STILLNESS IN YOUR LIFE

As I sat on that mountainside in Colorado, God began to unfold the meaning of the words *still* and *know* to me. He showed me how important these words are in the context of knowing Him.

Therefore, if we're going to understand what it means to be still and know God, we should take a closer look at what those two words mean.

The word *still* can literally be defined as "to abate, to cease, to let go, or to stop."[2] So, we could say being still includes letting go of the challenges, worries, and anxieties that encumber our lives. We could even broaden that definition to include the process of simplifying things in our lives. But, obviously, being still must involve more than that because we all know a lot of people who have ceased doing much of anything, and yet they don't know God.

In a similar sense, you can practice yoga or transcendental meditation, and you might get "still" in the sense of ceasing from worry or letting go of troubling things, but you're not going to know God that way. So there has to be another element involved in the definition of being still.

Now, as I was contemplating all of this, the Lord reminded me of another portion of Scripture in the Old Testament. Here's what He showed me:

> *Hast thou not known? hast thou not heard, that the everlasting God, the Lord, the Creator of the ends of the earth, fainteth not, neither is weary? there is no searching of his understanding. He giveth power to the faint; and to them that have no might he increaseth strength. Even the youths shall faint and be weary, and the young men shall utterly fall: But they that wait upon the Lord shall renew their strength; they shall mount up with wings as eagles; they shall run, and not be weary; and they shall walk, and not faint.*
>
> Isaiah 40:28-31

Notice that this verse says, "They that wait upon the Lord." Waiting on the Lord is related to being still and knowing that He is God. These two terms are related because, when they're combined, they conceptually give us a better understanding of what it means to be still.

The word *wait* here means "patient expectation." It means to patiently look for God, to patiently expect God.[3]

When we combine the concept of becoming still with the related concept of waiting expectantly on the Lord, we get an idea of what it means to cease from complications and distractions while patiently looking for God. We can move from looking at troubles to looking at the Lord. We move from focusing on the problem to focusing on the solution. To stillness, we've added an expectation that is looking for and focused on God.

WHAT IT MEANS TO KNOW GOD

As we've said before, to know God is the single most important thing anyone can ever do in life. The word *know* in Psalms 46:10 can be translated from the Hebrew to mean "to ascertain by seeing."[4]

How many of you have ever wanted to see God? Of course we all have. I've always wanted to see God. What a man or woman of faith it would make of us if we could see God. It would eliminate all the doubts, concerns, and little points of unbelief we may have. If we just saw Him like Thomas did, then we could know for sure that He is God, and there would never be any question. But the Lord told Thomas, "Blessed are they that have not seen, and yet have believed" (John 20:29).

It says in Psalms 46:10 that if we will be still before the Lord, we can make certain by seeing. That's what the word *know* in this verse means. We can ascertain His Godship in our lives by seeing!

Now, it may not be a literal seeing, an open vision, but the confirmation to our heart of His reality will be just as strong as if we were seeing God. The Bible says we can learn with certainty by seeing. You may have heard the old cliché, "Seeing is believing for an unbelieving world." Well, the Bible says we can have the same assurance that He is God as if we had actually seen Him with our own eyes!

Let's get down to some ways we can uncomplicate our lives and reach a place of stillness.

THE PROCESS OF SIMPLIFICATION

As the Lord told me on the side of that Colorado mountain, we can only know Him if we are "still." However, the god of this world, Satan, will try to make our lives so complex and so complicated that we can't receive the light or understanding that would otherwise come from the Word of God.

This is the primary reason most Christians don't truly know God. Their lives are just too complicated. It's not always a sin problem, or some great lack of knowledge, or even a hardness of heart that keeps them from truly knowing God and experiencing the transformation that comes with it. The main reason Christians aren't genuinely interested in God is that they are simply too stressed out. The result is that they end up practicing religion—a powerless form of godliness. (2 Timothy 3:5)

To be sure, it is a challenge to keep our lives simple enough to receive the light and understanding that God's Word will bring.

Knowing God is dependent upon our managing complications, eliminating them, and coming to a place where God can reveal Himself to us.

God doesn't make it hard to know Him. We can get to know Him through studying His Word and through communing with Him during times of prayer or fellowship.

However, if our minds are filled with the anxieties our complicated lives have produced, and if we're watching the clock while throwing out a five- or ten-minute prayer, we'll never really know God. We may know something about God, but that's not the same thing as knowing God Himself.

SIN COMPLICATES

Now, before we go any further, let me state that in a very basic sense, the presence of sin complicates our lives. Conversely, being obedient to God's Word simplifies our lives. In a very general way, we could accurately summarize things right now with that statement. But there are a few more things to say on the subject.

If you'll think about it for a moment, you'll see that sin of any sort complicates life. For example, when somebody gets involved in the sin of adultery, his or her life becomes imminently more complicated.

The lying, deception, and manipulation required to carry on the affair, not to mention the pain of broken relationships and broken homes, make the adulterer's life unbelievably complex and stressful.

Sin always complicates. It is much simpler to follow God's will and practice His Word.

But not everything that complicates our lives is a result of outright sin.

For example, when we study the seed principle found in God's Word, we'll find that sowing bad seed will produce bad fruit. If we were to sow seeds of laziness, for instance, we would end up reaping a pile of things that didn't get done. On the other hand, if we want good fruit, we must sow good seed because good seed produces nothing but good fruit.

Let me point out a physical truth. When you initially come into a lighted room after being in darkness or a deep shadow, you don't see very well for a moment or two. You'll squint because you're not accustomed to the brightness. However, within minutes your vision will come into focus.

The same thing is true spiritually. Even after a revelation from God initially comes, we may not be able to see or understand it fully at first.

The light of revelation tends to obscure our spiritual eyesight momentarily because we're not accustomed to it. Therefore, God says to continue in His Word so that we can see it more fully. (John 15:5) Many of us who hear the Word experience the illumination of God's light in an area of our lives that was otherwise dark, and naturally we begin to squint.

For example, when some people first hear that God wants to prosper them, they may squint a little in disbelief. Likewise, when some husbands first hear that they must love their wives as Christ loves the Church (Ephesians 5:25), they squint a little bit and say, "What now?"

There is a little illumination on the subject, but it's still probably not enough for them to see clearly.

Therefore, when you read or hear something that you don't understand, continue prayerfully searching the Scriptures, because God's truth will become clearer and more distinct as you continue in the Word.

NEEDFUL THINGS

There are many examples in the Bible of people who lived overly complicated lives. We can even see examples of people who were stressed out even though they spent time in the presence of Jesus Himself. Despite this advantage, some were not able to change. What happened? They missed the light and the understanding necessary to unravel their complicated circumstances. They never recognized the presence and power that existed right before them because they were too busy.

Let's look at a passage of Scripture that identifies one such person.

> Now it came to pass, as they went, that he [Jesus] entered into a certain village: and a certain woman named Martha received him into her house. And she had a sister called Mary, which also sat at Jesus' feet, and heard his word. But Martha was cumbered about much serving, and came to him, and said, Lord, dost thou not care that my sister hath left me to serve alone? bid her therefore that she help me. And Jesus answered and said unto her, Martha, Martha, thou art careful and trou-

bled about many things: But one thing is needful: and Mary hath chosen that good part, which shall not be taken away from her.

Luke 10:38-42

This passage reveals a lot about dealing with the complexities of life. Think about it. How many people have had the opportunity to sit at the feet of Jesus, learning from Him directly? Not many. Martha had that chance, and yet she couldn't benefit from it. Although she received Jesus into her house and served Him, she didn't receive the light from Him that could have changed her circumstances.

Things are much the same for Christians today. There are many believers who are hard-working, dedicated, committed servers in the house of the Lord. They receive Him, they love Him, and they serve Him, but they don't benefit from being in His presence.

Those things were all true for Martha, but there's something else that was true for her that's also true for many of us today. The Bible calls it being "cumbered about." In other words, Martha made things so complicated in her life that she couldn't get to the feet of Jesus to hear His Word.

Martha served in the presence of the Lord Jesus Christ Himself—something that many people today would give anything for the opportunity to do. But Martha wasn't choosing the best things in life. She wasn't being changed by the presence of the Lord.

To experience the transforming power of Jesus, we have to put some things aside, even though they may be good things.

If we want to know His presence and His power, we must simplify our lives, come to a place of stillness, and choose needful things.

Of course, serving God is a good thing, yet for Martha, it hindered her from hearing and receiving what Jesus wanted her to know.

Complications that befall us in life are obviously not always a result of sin. Martha certainly wasn't sinning as she served Jesus. Likewise, you and I can become involved in things that aren't sin either, yet which can encumber us and prevent us from receiving the light of God's Word. We need to measure our actions against the Word when we're deciding what is a complication in our lives.

I believe the writer of Hebrews had this truth in mind when he wrote:

> *Therefore, since we have so great a cloud of witnesses surrounding us, let us also lay aside every encumbrance, and the sin which so easily entangles us.*
>
> Hebrews 12:1 NAS

According to the verse, there is sin and there are encumbrances. Do you see it?

"But one thing is needful: and Mary hath chosen that good part, which shall not be taken away from her" (Luke 10:42).

In order to simplify your life, you must choose those things that are needful, as Mary did, instead of simply doing what would *seem* good or right to the natural mind. Choosing things that aren't needful will always produce cares and anxiety. (Luke 10:41)

Anytime you feel uptight or anxious about something, look to see if you're doing things that are not needful. Because doing things that are not necessary—even if they're good—will always produce complications somewhere.

Another indication that we've chosen something not needful is the presence of a critical disposition. Notice Martha's complaint to Jesus. She said, "Lord, dost thou not care that my sister has left me to serve alone? bid her therefore that she help me" (Luke 10:40).

Those who are encumbered with life's complications tend to be critical of others.

Martha loved Jesus, but she was complaining to Him about Mary. She served Him and even stood in His presence, doing things that seemed right to her. But the very fact that a critical spirit began to rise up in her against her sister—who seemed to be more blessed than she—was a warning sign that there were too many complications in her life. The very presence of criticism along with anxiety meant she needed to simplify her life.

It also indicated she was not sitting at the feet of Jesus. Unless we spend time at the feet of Jesus, we'll never know the Lord in the kind of life-changing way that makes religion personal instead of an empty ritual.

When we identify these earmarks of a complicated life, we must repent and turn back to God. Find that place of stillness and begin to simplify your life.

Obviously, we have responsibilities we can't ignore; there are things that must be addressed and attended to. Finding a place of stillness and simplifying our lives doesn't mean we should ignore our responsibilities. For example, we cannot just lay down our responsibilities at work so we can find a place of stillness. And we must not shirk our responsibilities as a spouse or parent for the sake of seeking God more. In fact, it doesn't mean we necessarily do anything suddenly or make any drastic changes. We can begin by prayerfully seeking God's direction under the guidance of the Holy Spirit. He will show us how to make changes in our behavior and actions that will begin the process of simplifying our lives.

MAKING GOOD CHOICES

"Mary hath chosen that good part, which shall not be taken away from her" (Luke 10:42). Jesus indicates that although Martha's choices were okay, they weren't the best. She could have made better choices that would have benefited her more and simplified her life. But notice, Jesus didn't *make* her choose differently.

Nobody can override your choices. Neither God nor Satan will *make* you choose something. You are responsible to choose things for yourself.

Since you have the responsibility for choosing, how do you choose the good part? The best way to make good choices is to measure your options against what God created you to be. Make choices that will help you fulfill your purpose and reject those choices that would encumber you and hinder you from reaching your destiny.

THREE

God's Managers

As we have seen, the obvious first step to take toward making life simpler is to focus on those things that contribute to our principal purpose in life.

All other distractions that don't add to life's principal purpose must be pared away. Define those goals and objectives that drive your life and let go of things that don't—even though they may be worthwhile or good. Fail to do that, and invariably, complications will come.

Each person's life goals are different, because everyone has a different call and an individual, divinely appointed destiny. Each of us has different gifts and callings, so each person must use his or her particular talents as he or she sees fit, according to God's will. It is vital to identify your God-ordained purpose, pare away the distractions, and focus on what's left.

We can also make life simpler by defining God's general purpose, which includes all of us.

We are in the Church age, and our purpose as believers in this dispensation is to preach the Gospel to all the world. (Matthew 28:19) Jesus told us to bring people into the house of

God, help them mature in the Word, and equip them so they can fulfill their ministries.

Every decision we make and everything we do with the resource of our time on this earth needs to be measured by this question: "Does what I'm doing contribute to these goals?" We need to ask ourselves, "Am I helping to get people saved, placed in a church, and grown up on the Word of God?" If we're not, then we're opening ourselves up for potential complications.

God has made various resources available to us. He's given us natural resources like time and money. He's given us spiritual gifts and talents, and He's given us helpful relationships with people who can share their skills and abilities with us. So when we think about it, we've got every resource God has available to help us fulfill His purpose for our lives.

NOT YOUR OWN

All the resources we're managing—including our own lives— are, first of all, God's property. This truth has great power to simplify our lives because in reality, we don't own anything.

Our resources are not really ours; they belong to God. They're not given for us to profit by nor have they been placed in our care so we can pursue our own agenda. It's not our stuff! And knowing that takes a big burden off our shoulders.

Everything is God's. We're stewards, or managers. We're here on this earth to manage life's resources on His behalf. This is the essence of what Paul said in 1 Corinthians 6:19,20:

Know ye not that...ye are not your own? For ye are bought with a price: therefore glorify God in your body, and in your spirit, which are God's.

So, the first perception change we have to embrace is that we're not in this for ourselves. We've been bought at the unimaginably high price of the blood of Jesus. Realizing this truth will help us avoid selfish motives. The moment self begins to drive our decision-making process, we're complicating and encumbering our lives. However, when we focus our concern on stewardship rather than on self, life will become less complex.

The stewardship calling is eternal, and managing on God's behalf now prepares us for our eternal rulership in heaven.

DEVELOP ORGANIZATIONAL SKILLS

Another way to simplify life is to become better managers of our lives.

Complication in any area can be a result of poor management.

Good management is nothing more than organizing the resources around us, to oversee something at our disposal in order to successfully accomplish a desired purpose. As God's managers, we are in charge of all of life's resources available to us.

Since God gave us the task of managing His kingdom on this earth, we are going to need some skills to accomplish that.

Some of us are better at organizing than others, but we're all required to skillfully take care of life's affairs. None of us are exempt from our own responsibilities of stewardship.

But God doesn't call us to do something without giving us a way to do it, telling us *how* to do it, and *equipping* us to do it. We might not even recognize it as organization, but we're doing it all the time. For example, whenever we pay our bills and balance our checkbook, we're organizing. Every time we plan a meal and cook it, we're organizing. Organization can be defined as merely putting things into a working order.

Nobody can organize or manage the affairs of our lives better than we can, and that includes our spouse, our best friend, or our boss. We must see ourselves as God sees us and understand that we do have the ability and responsibility to organize the affairs of our own lives.

FOUR

Effective Organization

As I stated previously, one of our goals is to find a place of stillness in order to know the Lord more fully.

We've looked at ways we can simplify things, and one way is to choose needful things as Mary did.

We've also learned that the way to begin the process of simplifying our life is to align our activities with our God-given purpose.

Since we're all called to be stewards, or God's managers, we know our goal is to do that job well by becoming organized.

Let's go back to where we started in Psalms 119:130 and notice two words—*understanding* and *simple*.

> *The entrance of thy words giveth light; it giveth understanding unto the simple.*
>
> Psalms 119:130

The gaining of understanding is dependent upon the existence of a simplified life. I believe understanding cannot exist where there are complications.

I think it is fair to say then that the things God says lead to understanding indicate that they would have the effect of simplifying our lives.

What does understanding mean then?

We see the term *understanding* frequently used in the Old Testament, especially in the book of Proverbs. In fact, the word *understanding* appears in the book of Proverbs over forty times, and most of those times it is used in association with two other words—*wisdom* and *knowledge.*

Therefore, if we can understand the relationship between wisdom, knowledge, and understanding, then we can get a better idea of the word *understanding* and learn how to cultivate it.

Understanding is the link between knowledge and wisdom. We can't apply the knowledge we have without understanding. The only way knowledge can become wisdom is through the channel of understanding. So understanding becomes an important concept.

Take a look at a few verses in Proverbs that use all three words together.

> *Through wisdom is a house builded; and by understanding it is established: and by knowledge shall the chambers be filled with all precious and pleasant riches.*

Proverbs 24:3,4

All three words are used in such a way as to give us a basic idea of the meaning of each. I define the word *knowledge* as the acquisition of information, facts, and data. If you were to check a concordance, you would find that the root word means to know by observation, reflection, or experience.[1]

The presence of knowledge is only the first step, and it must be combined with wisdom to be useful and beneficial.

We can see from Proverbs 24:3 that wisdom is applied knowledge: "Through wisdom is a house builded." Knowledge is the foundation, but wisdom is the structure. Wisdom is the ability to make knowledge produce the desired result.

For example, you may take classes in physics and memorize complex mathematical formulas but still never make it work for you. Perhaps it's only if you become a scientist and are able to apply the empirical data that these laws begin to produce and work for you. Otherwise, you just have a lot of knowledge but no ability to use it.

Remember, understanding is the connection between knowledge and wisdom.

I define the word *understanding* as "to mentally organize."

To have understanding is to possess the ability to mentally organize gathered information and arrange it into a functional relationship with the other information already acquired so that it fits together in the best or most correct way.

Very simply, understanding is the process of mentally organizing any given resource at your disposal.

The good news is that God will give you all the wisdom and understanding you need if you ask Him for it. (James 1:5)

With that in mind, let's look at some Scriptures that use the word *understanding.*

I went by the field of the slothful, and by the vineyard of the man void of understanding; and, lo, it was all grown over with thorns, and nettles had covered the face thereof, and the stone wall thereof was broken down.

Proverbs 24:30,31

Notice that it is the person void of understanding who suffers from a life that is overrun by complications (thorns, nettles, and broken walls). A lack of understanding produces this kind of chaos.

We use these kinds of examples to preach, "Don't be lazy! Because if you're lazy, your life will be chaotic, unsuccessful, and unfruitful." And it's true, we will become slothful about natural and spiritual things if we don't cultivate understanding.

But notice these verses talk about two different categories of people whose lives produce the same fruit. Both the slothful person and the person void of understanding—or the unorganized person—suffer the same calamity. Both have fields overgrown with thorns and nettles.

One who is void of understanding will suffer the same consequences as someone who is slothful.

One who doesn't take the resources of his or her life and put them into meaningful, functional categories will get into trouble. The unorganized person produces the same fruit as the lazy, slothful person. The fruit from each is failure and chaos.

One of the Hebrew words translated *understanding* in the Old Testament *(biyn)* is associated with the process of mentally organizing the knowledge and information at your disposal.

That's why it's so absolutely essential that we organize our resources so that we can simplify our lives.

Look at another Scripture verse that deals with the subject of organizational ability: "How much better is it to get wisdom than gold! and to get understanding rather to be chosen than silver!" (Proverbs 16:16).

Both silver and gold are precious metals. If wisdom is analogous to gold and understanding is like silver, then getting understanding is only slightly less valuable than wisdom. The ability to mentally organize the facts and data of our lives into functional arrangements is only second to the ability to make knowledge work on our behalf.

Furthermore, understanding is a steppingstone to wisdom. The thing that really stands out in Proverbs 16:16 and other scriptures in the book of Proverbs is that the phrases *get wisdom* and *get understanding* often appear together.

God is telling us we need to get wisdom, *and* we need to get understanding. Well, if we're told to get it, that means it must be available to us. We just need to know how to acquire organizational skills and apply them to the areas of our greatest need.

MEDITATE ON GOD'S WORD

God tells us to get understanding because we must have understanding to simplify our lives. Look at Psalm 119:99. "I have more understanding than all my teachers." Why? The last part of the verse tells us: "For thy testimonies are my meditation."

If we want to cultivate the organizational ability inherent in every believer, then we must meditate on God's Word. God created us to function with the ability to organize our own life. And the tool He gave us to accomplish that task is called "meditation." Meditating on God's Word is the beginning point in the process of becoming an organized person.

To meditate means, very basically, to conjure a mental image of something or to ponder or consider a matter.

Too many people lead complicated, frustrating lives. Though they may have an abundance of resources at their disposal, they have never gathered them into a functional order. Their knowledge has never been put to use to produce an organized end result. Understanding hasn't come. These people haven't mentally separated and arranged all available resources into an organized whole.

That's why God tells us to get understanding. Five times in the books of Psalms and Proverbs He says, "Get understanding." Understanding is not a gift that's reserved only for a special few. It's available to anyone who will take the time to cultivate it.

Psalm 119:99 can also be paraphrased this way: *I have more organizational ability than all my teachers, because God's Word is my meditation.*

The ability to organize comes through meditating on God's Word. The ability of the human brain to produce imagery in the mind is a necessary step toward the simplified life.

Psalm 49:3 says, "My mouth shall speak of wisdom; and the meditation of my heart shall be of understanding." Wisdom is the product of a heart full of understanding.

Meditation involves visual imagery, pondering, and considering all the facts at our disposal. They may be facts from God's Word, or they may be natural facts. But the point is, we are meditating for the purpose of putting these facts into a functional arrangement.

Most unorganized people fall into one of two categories—non-meditators and daydreamers. As a result, they wonder why their lives are so complicated.

These same people are the ones who bolt out of bed in the morning with barely enough time to put on their britches. All they eat is a piece of toast on the way out the door. Oh, they say a few "Hallelujahs" and "Thank You, Fathers," calling it their devotional time, but it's pinched and rushed. Then, when they encounter their first obstacle of the day, they just deal with it as it comes. They haven't arranged, organized, or planned anything.

God has a better way.

I used to call this process of meditation "creative thought." But whatever you call it, this is what goes on when you mentally arrange the information and data into the most functional arrangement possible to accomplish a desired goal. Only then will you simplify your life.

Meditating is part of the process of simplifying your life. We must give time to it and be sure to keep our thought life diligently applied to the task at hand. Don't mentally wander off to your golf game or daydream about something else.

It's a challenge, but this is where the process of organization begins.

Let me warn you about something. Meditation is not sitting back and letting your thoughts drift and wander. Furthermore, meditation isn't synonymous with prayer or with praising God, interceding for others, or making your supplications known. Those are important parts of prayer, but they are very different activities.

To be sure, our time with the Lord is crucially important, but we must set aside additional time to meditate on God's Word. Here is what God said about meditating.

> *This book of the law shall not depart out of thy mouth; but thou shalt meditate therein day and night, that thou mayest observe to do according to all that is written therein: for then thou shalt make thy way prosperous, and then thou shalt have good success.*
>
> Joshua 1:8

In the process of organizing, acquiring knowledge is the first step. We must hear the Word and keep it in our mouth so we can refresh our own heart and hopefully someone else's. But after we hear the Word, we must meditate on all the available information concerning the subject, because that leads to understanding. That's the way you mentally embrace, arrange, and organize your resources until you understand their proper relationship to one another.

For example, we've heard that Jesus heals, but hearing that doesn't automatically mean there is understanding in the area of healing. Hearing that Jesus heals is really not enough information to obtain a healing for yourself. Don't get me wrong; it's a good start. But simply knowing that Jesus heals doesn't mean you've acquired enough knowledge to put things into a meaningful, functional arrangement so that this truth can begin to work in your life.

You must gain more knowledge in addition to hearing the words *Jesus heals* to assimilate the subject of healing into your life.

You need to find out that being healed by Jesus is a redemptive benefit; He paid a price to heal everyone; by His stripes you were healed; and it's God's will to heal everybody. Once you've acquired these additional facts on the subject of healing, you're better prepared to understand and believe that Jesus heals.

Acquire a little more information on the subject of healing, and you'll find that healing can be communicated by the laying on of hands or anointing with oil. And, if you dig a little deeper into the subject, you'll discover that you must have faith to receive healing. Using faith appropriates healing. As you continue your search, you'll also find that faith without works is dead. You're going to need a corresponding action in addition to your faith.

Once you've obtained all of this information on the subject of healing, you need to meditate on it until all the pieces start to fall into place. Pretty soon the light comes on, and you go forward until you receive your healing.

This illustrates the process of gathering information or data from all the resources available and applying them until a desired result is achieved.

It's important to allow time to think about these things, to ponder them, and to mull them over. Meditation helps you do this.

I do this all the time, whether it's with a promise of God, finances, or human resources. I'm constantly giving time to considering the resources around me.

For example, when it comes to the management of human resources, I'm always thinking about and imagining the best possible scenarios for my staff. I often ask myself, "Are there enough of them? And, if so, are they in the right place to use their talents and skills?" What am I doing when I do this? I'm meditating on the resources available to me.

Meditation is where we begin. This is how we cultivate understanding, and it's how we become organized.

THE HOLY SPIRIT IS YOUR HELPER

We're not alone in our quest to become organized. There's Someone who wants to help us, so don't be dismayed. "Trust in the Lord with all thine heart; and lean not unto thine own understanding" (Proverbs 3:5).

Don't get so caught up with your own organizational challenges that you become overwhelmed. *You have the gift!* You can organize anything, because the Holy Spirit is helping you.

On more than one occasion I've encountered the misconception that people think they have to do this all alone. But
that's simply not true. We could read Proverbs 3:5 the following way: *Don't lean to your own organizational ability.* That's
good news!

Isaiah says there's Someone with the gift of understanding
to help you:

> *And the spirit of the Lord shall rest upon him, the spirit of*
> *wisdom and understanding, the spirit of counsel and might, the*
> *spirit of knowledge and of the fear of the Lord.*
>
> Isaiah 11:2

That's a promise to us!

The Spirit of understanding is the Holy Spirit of God who
lives on the inside of you. He's called the Spirit of understanding because it is part of His responsibility to help us organize
our lives. We never need to feel that we don't have the ability
to become organized because we are the temple of the chief
organizer Himself! We've got the head organizer living in us,
and His job is to help us organize every facet of our lives.

I can't imagine starting a day without turning to the Holy
Spirit to help me get organized. I turn to Him in the morning,
asking for His guidance as I plan my day. I start by meditating
on the resource at hand, whether it be the Word of God, time
management, human resources, or financial resources. Then I
begin praying in tongues, stirring up the ministry of the Holy
Spirit inside me. I would be lost if I didn't do this.

You will gain an advantage if you'll pray in tongues as you plan your day, because you're yielding to His ministry. That's all tongues is. When you pray in tongues, you're saying, "Lord, I recognize the indwelling presence of the Holy Spirit in my life."

I pray in tongues, or in the Spirit, because I don't always know how to pray as I ought to. But I know the Holy Spirit knows. He helps me understand the areas of greatest need and how to answer them.

All of the information at your disposal will become meaningful as you meditate on God's Word and pray in the Holy Spirit. You'll be able to formulate a plan and see how to execute it. As you sit there praying in the Holy Spirit and meditating on the resources at hand, you will become the most organized person around.

Most people don't believe they have time to stop and meditate. The truth is, they don't have time *not* to. I got an amusing reminder of that truth not too long ago. I scheduled a couple of big meetings close together on the calendar but far apart geographically.

It was a busy week, and I had a lot of clothes to pack. But this was an easy task for me because I had thoroughly organized my packing technique. I gave a lot of thought to it. I took all of the resources at hand there in my closet, thought it through, put it all together in a meaningful, functional relationship, and got my clothes into one bag.

My wife, on the other hand, came in from prayer, hadn't thought a moment about what she wanted to take, and she ended up packing fourteen bags. She took everything! Instead of thinking about what she needed to wear beforehand, she took everything in her closet so she could decide what to wear when she got there. She claims that her way is good because she doesn't ever forget anything. (How could she? She takes everything!)

The point is, you organize what you think about. What you give your thought life to is the area you'll be organized in, because organization is, first of all, a mental process.

Have you ever noticed that there are many things you don't like to think about? Usually, those are the areas in your life that have gotten complicated. For instance, if there's a relationship that's become complex, perhaps due to anger and contention, chances are you need to give some thought to the source of the problem. Ask yourself, "Where is this conflict coming from?"

That's not always a pleasant thing to think about. However, when there's a problem area in your life, you need to spend time meditating and thinking about godly solutions, letting God show you how to better manage that problem. Instead of neglecting those areas that most need it, you should get God involved and find a solution. Then begin to properly manage the neglected areas.

Another thing people usually don't like to think about are financial problems. When someone gets into a financial mess, when creditors begin calling and bills begin piling up, it's often easier to just ignore the debt, the bills, and the creditors, but that's not wise.

We don't like to think about such things, but that's exactly what we need to meditate on and pray about in the Holy Spirit, then ask God to give us a plan that will solve the problem.

On the other hand, those things we like to think about are usually the things in which we are most organized.

Take my wife's prayer ministry, for example. She has organized that group down to the gnat's eyebrow, because she loves to think about it!

When it comes to my flying (I'm a pilot with a background in the Air Force and the aviation industry), I'm thoroughly organized. I don't go up in an airplane without getting all my stuff together first. I enjoy planning a trip; therefore, I'm very organized about it.

Do you see the link between thought and organization? The things we think about most are the areas where we're the most organized, the most functional, the most simplified, and running the smoothest. The areas to which we give little thought, planning, and prayer are the areas where our lives become complicated and stressful.

God wants us to use our brains, but He also wants us to use His. It's a partnership, and He's here to help us simplify our problem areas.

Planning a Time-Management Strategy

Like most believers, you probably want to know God better and you've discovered that to know Him better, you need to simplify your life. But standing between you and that glorious goal are distractions that come in the form of demands on your time.

Time may be the most important of the three primary resources. Why? Because there's only so much of it. Unlike money and relationships, when it's gone, it's gone.

Every person on the face of the earth—rich and poor, educated and ignorant, lost and saved—only gets 1,440 minutes per day. Time is the ultimate scarce resource.

Therefore, it's critical that we find out what we're called to do in order to make the most of the time we have available. If you don't know specifically what God has called you to do, don't panic. God has a unique calling for everyone that will incorporate each of our gifts, talents, abilities, and personalities. And He'll show you what your calling is if you ask Him.

If we can organize our time well, then we can organize our lives. That's really all life is—the passage of time for an individual. And, of course, we want the passage of time in our lives to be rich, productive, and full of meaning.

Ephesians 5:15-16 admonishes, "See then that ye walk circumspectly, not as fools, but as wise, redeeming the time, because the days are evil."

I also like *The Amplified Bible's* translation of these same verses:

> *Look carefully then how you walk! Live purposefully and worthily and accurately, not as the unwise and witless, but as wise (sensible, intelligent people), making the very most of the time [buying up each opportunity], because the days are evil.*
>
> Ephesians 5:15,16 Amp.

God is telling us that if we don't do something He calls "redeeming the time," then our days are going to potentially be filled with Satan's purpose, with the evil and the corruption that's a part of this world. The word *evil* means "hurtful" or "calamitous"; in other words, not good or fruitful.

The reason our days will become unfruitful is very simple. The Bible says that Satan is the god of this world, but God never intended it to be this way. God delegated His power, His dominion, and His authority to Adam, instructing him to manage the earth on His behalf. But Adam committed treason by disobeying God's commandment and wound up giving that dominion and authority to Satan.

Satan is the prince of the power of the air, and, as such, he has the legal right to try to manipulate people and circumstances to accomplish his will, which is to produce evil on the earth. But believers don't have to let him do that.

Sometimes, we mistakenly get the idea that God will just do whatever He pleases on the earth. While it's true that God is omnipotent, He chooses to operate through human vessels. He delegated dominion of this earth to man back in the Garden of Eden, and He is a God of His Word. That's a limitation He's imposed on Himself. And barring miracles, He can only do what we will cooperate on with Him.

So, for the duration of this age, we must do something to redeem the time, because the days are filled with evil instead of good.

BUYING BACK LOST TIME

"To redeem" means to buy back something that is lost. In this context, our time is lost and virtually unproductive unless we spend it becoming an efficient time manager.

Well, how much does time cost? Look again at the text in Ephesians.

> *See then that ye walk circumspectly, not as fools, but as wise, redeeming the time, because the days are evil. Wherefore be ye not unwise, but* understanding *what the will of the Lord is.*
>
> Ephesians 5:15-17

Isn't it beautiful how the Word flows together? God is saying that to buy back time, we must spend time meditating— mentally separating, organizing, and arranging the facts at hand—to understand the will of the Lord. The price we have to pay to redeem time is paid in time. It's time spent meditating

43

on the Word and all the other resources in our lives that will help us make good choices. If we don't invest that time wisely, we won't redeem any time. Consequently, our days will end up ill spent, unfruitful, or evil.

This is why many Christians continue to experience setbacks when they could be experiencing victory. God's children have been redeemed, and so has their time. A believer's life is his or her time. But it's going to take some investing to walk in that redemption. It's one thing to be redeemed, but it's another thing to walk it out.

PLANNING YOUR TIME WISELY

Any good time-management strategy begins with a good planning phase. If you're going to manage your time well, you're going to need a plan.

To have a good time-management plan, you'll need to incorporate three useful tools. The first tool you'll need is something we've already talked about—meditation. But I want to look at the subject of meditation from a different angle so you can have a good grasp of what you're doing when you sit down to meditate.

First of all, I want to emphasize that I'm not talking about the mystical, New Age type of meditation that is part of so many Eastern religious practices. When I say meditation, I mean the biblical kind of meditation that centers on God's Word and His principles.

BUILDING MIND PICTURES

We already know that to meditate means "to make a mental image of something, to build mind pictures," and that this should be a daily process. (Ephesians 5:16)

We already know that meditating promotes organization and is the first contributor to the successful planning of a time-management strategy. It's mentally building pictures of what we want our day to be like.

A really good example of this came to me years ago while I was reading an article about NASA, the National Aeronautics and Space Administration. According to the article, NASA was designing a vehicle that would be used to explore planets where the atmosphere isn't capable of supporting human life. The article described how a rocket would transport a space vehicle to a planet, negotiate a landing, and finally discharge a vehicle designed for surface exploration. It would look like the lunar rover that explored the moon, only it would be completely enclosed with its own internally controlled environment that could keep the astronauts safe while they explored the planet. They would navigate by using external sensors to project an image of the planet's surface onto a screen inside the vehicle.

It occurred to me after I read the article that the image of the terrain had to be clear enough for the explorers to navigate the planet. Suppose, for example, that the astronauts in the space vehicle had to navigate the unexplored terrain with all its cliffs, ravines, and other obstacles without the benefit of a clear viewing screen. Could they successfully navigate while using a fuzzy screen that showed a blurred vision of their surroundings? No, they wouldn't be able to see anything. They might accidentally run off a cliff, or drive into a crater. Obviously, instead of risking this kind of danger, they would wait until they had a clear picture of what lay ahead. Only after a clear image came into focus would they proceed.

Well, the same is true for us. How many of us start out without a clear picture of what the day is supposed to look like? We blunder through the day, falling off cliffs, and dropping into craters, when all we needed was a clear image of what the day should look like.

Meditation time is intended to focus the picture of your day. Building mind pictures clearly defines the image of your time so you can navigate your day with purpose and precision. Remember that Ephesians 5:17 in *the Amplified Bible* it says we're to live purposefully, worthily, and accurately.

I practice biblical meditation on a daily basis, but I also like to mentally build clear pictures on the first day of each week. I meditate, framing images not only about that day, but also about the days ahead. Then at the beginning of each month, I also cover not only the coming day and week, but also the coming months.

I don't know how God may deal with you to do it, but you need to build pictures of your life that will guide you as you navigate your day. Picture a plan of success and see yourself walking it out until it becomes a reality.

First you picture it; then you live it.

SELECTION MAKES PERFECTION

The second major contributor or tool to planning a successful time-management strategy is something I call "selectivity."

Do you remember the Bible's description of Martha doing a lot of good things that nevertheless prevented her from receiving from Jesus? She did so many good things that she didn't have time to sit at His feet to experience His presence or receive the direction He would bring.

Martha needed to be more selective. Had she employed the principle of selectivity, then she would have made some good choices like Mary did and would have been seated at Jesus' feet alongside Mary, enjoying the presence of God.

Every day of your life you're going to have the opportunity to do a lot of good things, maybe even needful things. But if you don't cultivate the habit of selectivity—being selective in the planning phase of your day—you'll never have enough hours to do everything you want to do. Your life will become so complicated, you won't even want to get up in the morning!

Philippians 1:10 puts it this way: "That ye may approve things that are excellent." I also like *The Amplified Bible*'s rendering of this scripture. It says, "So that you may surely learn to sense what is vital, and approve and prize what is excellent and of real value [recognizing the highest and the best]."

God tells us we must be discriminating and selective in choosing how to spend our time. We must incorporate that into the planning phase of our time-management strategy. We simply can't do everything. Our lives would be a mess if we tried.

We could do a lot of good things with our time and still live a complicated life, so we must choose the most important things.

We need to be aware of the scriptural priorities God outlines in His Word. There are some things that God plainly tells us are more important than others. For example, our relationship with Him is to be paramount. Everything about our lives hinge on our fellowship with God.

Sadly, spending time with God is usually the first thing most people cut when their days begin to get complicated. They either completely cut out their time with God, or they cut it down to an insignificant fragment of time. It's no wonder people suffer from overly complicated lives.

Remember, the time we spend with God in prayer, in the Word, and in worshiping Him is different from meditating. There is a time to meditate, arrange the facts of our day, pray in the Holy Spirit, and allow the Spirit of understanding to help us organize our day. But our first priority is to commune with the Lord.

Next to God, our highest priority is our spouse. If you're married, you'll need to dedicate meaningful time to your wife or husband in the process of selectivity, or you'll have problems. You can't neglect your spouse and expect to lead a simplified life. It just won't happen.

The next priority in the process of selectivity is your children.

Be selective about time spent with your husband or wife, then your children, and then your ministry. Put your family before your ministry and involvement with the church. After attending to these responsibilities, give time to your vocation and lastly to your recreation time.

Although recreation is last on the list of priorities, that doesn't mean it's not important. God wants us to plan recreation time. That's the will of God for us, because He doesn't want us to become old, dry, boring nobodies. He wants us to enjoy life. God has given us all things richly to enjoy, but if we don't schedule recreational events in our day or week, we'll never enjoy them. As a result, we'll risk burnout.

DELEGATE YOUR DUTIES

The third major contributor or tool to planning a successful time-management strategy is to know how to delegate. To delegate means to assign potentially time-consuming duties to someone capable of taking care of them. Delegation is crucial to a successful time-management strategy.

Obviously, we can't do everything ourselves, even if we're being selective about what we do, so we must learn to delegate some duties to others. When we release ourselves from some responsibilities, we free ourselves to do other things.

Sometimes that isn't easy to do. Some people may feel threatened by the idea of giving up some of their responsibilities, but they shouldn't.

Delegating certain duties to someone else is a necessary part of simplifying your life. Not only that, but delegating part of your responsibilities to others develops a healthy work ethic.

Hoarding responsibilities can be an act of pride or fear. If you're afraid to let go of some of your duties, you should examine your motives. Don't be afraid to let someone else share in your know-how. Likewise, don't let pride prevent you from allowing someone else to know what you know. You can't possibly do all the things required of you in any given day; so relax and train someone else to do your job.

Have you ever wondered what makes the best kind of business manager? The best business manager is the best delegator. The worst thing a manager can do is try to do everything him- or herself.

Unfortunately, I see this all the time. I saw it in my own business, and I see it in the ministry.

I've seen men and women who are gung-ho, going up the corporate ladder and getting promoted, but along the way they never learn to delegate. They try to do everything themselves, and the next thing you know, they're working twenty hours a day. They haven't seen their spouses in a month or two, and their families are going down the drain. Their lives are crumbling.

The best managers are the best delegators because they are fulfilling two requirements: training people to accept more responsibility and freeing their own time so they can be more creative.

Remember the story of Moses and Jethro in the Bible? Moses was trying to do all the work of judging his people by himself. Jethro finally had to step in and say, "The way you're doing this is not good." (Exodus 18:17) And Moses listened. He stopped trying to judge the multitude of problems alone. He delegated his job to others who were capable, and it solved his problem.

Everybody has someone they can delegate some of their overwhelming responsibilities to. That doesn't mean you give away all your duties and just loaf all day. You're not delegating to avoid doing your own work or to take advantage of someone else's goodwill. That would be wrong.

Delegating occurs when everyone pulls his or her own weight. When the whole family is working together, it's all right for the wife to ask her husband to help with the dishes or to pick the kids up from school. Likewise, husbands should be able to count on their wives to help with errands or bookkeeping. The Bible calls for believers to submit one to another. (Ephesians 5:21)

Don't overlook your children in the delegation process. You need to delegate to your kids because it's an important part of the training process. If you have kids, put them to work when they reach a reasonable age. For example, have them do the dishes, vacuum the rugs, or mow the lawn. This will simplify your life and, at the same time, train your kids to successfully handle the responsibilities of life.

It's interesting to know that delegating is not a secular idea. In fact, Paul often delegated his responsibilities when he couldn't perform them himself. Paul delegated to Timothy, Titus, and Barnabas, just to name a few. Paul would send them to the churches he had started with this message: *Hey, I couldn't come myself, but receive your brother, my servant in the*

Lord, on my behalf, because he didn't have time to go to all those places himself.

PLAN YOUR DAY FOR SUCCESS

We all begin each day with a finite number of hours, so we must have faith that God will help us use our time wisely. He's the One who designed the twenty-four-hour period, but it's up to us to manage it properly with His help. During those twenty-four hours, we all need time to sleep, time to eat, and time to maintain our bodies. We'll never get so spiritual as to rise above these basic needs.

I'm amazed at the stories I hear from some people I meet. For instance, I bumped into a guy who actually hadn't slept in two weeks. He said the Holy Spirit was refreshing him so he could pray around the clock. Boy! When I heard that, my mouth dropped open. But, bless his heart, he received some gentle correction and got back on track before his mind and body gave out completely.

Since there are certain things that aren't optional, we must allocate an appropriate amount of time for them. If we do them according to God's design and principles, we'll be blessed. We can keep sicknesses and diseases away and even keep the aging process from accelerating too quickly. That means as we age, we may require a little more sleep. An important part of time management is being sure to get enough rest. God rested, and so should we.

If we spend seven hours sleeping and one hour eating, that leaves us sixteen hours for other things. Most management "gurus" or consultants would warn against scheduling more than 80 percent of our available time to accommodate any unplanned contingencies or emergencies that may occur. That means we should leave three unscheduled hours out of twenty-four. Now, out of those thirteen hours usually comes a minimum of eight hours dedicated to work.

Don't forget work. The Bible says, "The labour of the righteous tendeth to life" (Proverbs 10:16). It's the will of God that we work, and if we're living in America today, that means we're working about eight hours minimum every day. After working eight hours a day, that leaves five hours left over. So we can see how important our time becomes when we break it down this way.

Another major consideration that we must factor into our schedules is time spent taking care of our bodies. We need to exercise and take care of the Holy Spirit's temple. I usually blend my meditation time with my exercise time. I use exercise and meditation with God together because I can do both without compromising either. Sometimes I can run while I listen to my Walkman with a tape of the Word playing. Other times, I work out in my house while watching a video of somebody preaching. And still other times, I just play praise music and worship the Lord while I work out. Exercise lends itself to this kind of activity.

Beware of the television. It's potentially a huge time waster. Some surveys have shown that the average American spends four hours a day watching television, and some children spend as many as six!

I want to pose a question. If you're prone to watching two or three hours of TV a night, where do you get the time to do other things? And you wonder why your life gets so complicated. There just isn't room for that kind of distraction.

There certainly will be days when we may have to use our flextime, or unscheduled time, to wind down. And there may be other times when we need to spend some time, for example, reading recreationally or watching a good TV program. There's nothing wrong with that, especially if you're watching a program on which the Word is being preached, rather than watching junk.

I can remember one season of time when my wife, Lynne, really got into this time-management thing. At the beginning, she had her whole day all laid out. There wasn't one minute that wasn't planned and accounted for. The funny thing is that she didn't plan for contingencies.

Back then we had a cockatiel named Moses. I hated that bird. I don't think he cared for me either because he would bite me. (Talk about biting the hand that feeds you!)

At that time, we stored Moses' birdseed in the refrigerator to keep it fresh. That worked well until one of the kids left the big sack of birdseed sitting right on the edge of the shelf. One day Lynne opened the refrigerator door, on schedule I might add, and *bang!* The sack fell out and birdseed scattered all over the kitchen floor, into the dining room, and even into the living room. What an unscheduled mess!

That almost did Lynne in. She came close to quitting her time-management plan right then.

You might laugh (I did), but that's the feeling you can have when you run too tight a time-management schedule and don't allow for contingencies. If we don't provide for some flex in our schedule, when something unexpected happens, it can make us want to throw in the towel.

We don't need to be dogmatic about scheduling our time. Just remember to use some commonsense knowledge and follow the three factors for successfully planning a time-management strategy—meditation, selectivity, and delegation. Follow these basic steps, and God will honor your efforts. He'll be faithful to help you redeem the time.

IMPLEMENTING A TIME-MANAGEMENT STRATEGY

If ever God needed to speak to His people about simplifying their lives, it would be now. The information age has brought with it some crushing demands. This challenge makes it difficult to manage anything anymore, but with a good time-management strategy, it is very possible to get control of a busy life.

People frequently ask me why they don't see God's glory, His presence, or His anointing. They often ask, "Why don't I experience these things when others seem to have it happen to them regularly?"

The answer I tell them is that they must become skilled at simplifying their lives in order for God's Word to bring light and understanding.

I believe this is one of the main reasons some people who love God and want to know Him more can come to church and never experience that flash of light and understanding that God's Word brings.

Planning a time-management strategy is only the first step. The second step is to implement that strategy.

Implementing it is a different challenge. It's one thing to have a plan, but it's another thing to put your plan to work for you. You could be a wonderful planner, but if you're not careful, you could lose it all when it comes to the implementation phase.

GET SINGLE-MINDED

Be determined and single-minded in the pursuit of your plan. Do not allow yourself to get detoured, distracted, or interrupted. These things can push you off course, preventing you from finishing your plan.

Sometimes I get accused of being inflexible when it comes to following my schedule. However, if I'm not absolutely determined and single-minded about accomplishing it, I won't get any of it done. The alternative to being single-minded is being double-minded, and you know what James says about that: "A double minded man is unstable in all his ways" (James 1:8).

Distractions come in many sizes and shapes. For example, consider the ringing of the telephone. Although the telephone can be a wonderful instrument of communication, it can also be a major distraction. If we don't manage our time on the telephone, we'll never get our plan for the day accomplished.

It can really be tough sometimes. Those calls come in from people we love who want to chat about wonderful moves of God or the great things that happened in church the night before. And then before we know it, an hour is gone! And though we were talking about important things, it was still a distraction.

So instead of answering all your calls, you could decide to let some go to the answering machine. But that could be a mistake. I sometimes suspect that answering machines are from the devil, because the messages pile up and most of us feel obligated to call everyone back! You know what a typical greeting says: "Leave a message at the beep, and I'll call you back." Well, that's just great! Now you've given your word that you'll call all of those people back. You don't have a choice. And there could be fourteen messages on your machine! There goes your day.

Perhaps a more honest greeting on your answering machine should say something like this: "Leave a message at the beep, and *maybe* somebody will call you back. But don't count on it. I'll get back to you if I have time."

Of course, this is making light of the situation, but the point is that if we don't take charge of the telephone, it will take charge of us.

I have always been pretty serious about managing distractions caused by the telephone. In fact, I went through a phase during the growth period of our ministry when the telephone really got to be distracting to me. This troubled me because our small staff was losing valuable time to the telephone. Then I came up with a simple solution that solved the problem.

I bought a handful of those three-minute hourglass timers and put one next to the telephone on everybody's desk. This did not make me very popular, and I received a lot of teasing for doing it. But the important thing is that it worked.

Whenever that phone would ring, I would just go over and start the timer. Then, when three minutes were up, it was time to get off the call.

This little trick did wonders for our time management. It didn't make for very many detailed phone conversations, but it sure saved a lot of time. All there was time for was getting down to the basics.

You see, all too often Christians are afraid to say, "No, I'm sorry. I can't talk now. We'll have to schedule a time later for this." For many of us, that's difficult to do, but people who love and respect each other should also love and respect one another's time. Managing time well allows the light and understanding from God to come.

You might begin thinking about your time drainers and remember that Satan will do everything he can to deter you from accomplishing the will of God, but you don't have to let him. Be determined to see your plan through.

ENERGY CONSERVATION

In the natural, there are only two reasons we might not see our plans through—distractions or lack of motivation.

Sometimes our energy reserves get depleted long before our day is over. We may find ourselves, for example, lacking the sufficient "oomph" to make it through to the end of the day. I see this a lot.

I talk to some people who just sit there while I'm talking, and I can tell their mind is a thousand miles away. They've had it. Their energy has been sapped. They might as well have gone home at one o'clock for all the good they did that afternoon.

In the secular arena, this is something called "tension anxiety," which is simply stress. Stress is not something new. Both the Bible and the world agree that stress is bad. God puts it this way: "Don't take cares upon yourself; instead, cast them on Me." (1 Peter 5:7) Moreover, secular professionals agree that excessive stress is detrimental to your health and is the greatest energy drain in the workplace.

Of course, as believers, we have an advantage over the secular world. We have the Word and God's Holy Spirit to help us combat stress. God's Word puts it the following way:

> *Hast thou not known? hast thou not heard, that the everlasting God, the Lord, the Creator of the ends of the earth, fainteth not, neither is weary? there is no searching of his understanding. He giveth power to the faint; and to them that have no might he increaseth strength. Even the youths shall faint and be weary, and the young men shall utterly fall: But they that wait upon the Lord shall renew their strength; they shall mount up with wings as eagles; they shall run, and not be weary; and they shall walk, and not faint.*
>
> Isaiah 40:28-31

This is God's answer for the stress and anxiety that so commonly drain energy and divert good intentions. God always reminds His people to cast their stress on Him, and He will renew their strength.

Remember, we said that "to wait" in the Hebrew means "to expect or look for." We need to expect the Lord to come through for us. We need to look for the Lord to give us the resource of strength to get us through the day. Expect Him to take care of any circumstances that are potentially draining.

Get rid of the idea that your success depends solely on you. Realize that you're a steward for God, not for yourself. Therefore, it's His problem. You're just His hands and feet in this process of His plan. It's not your care; it's His.

Expect and look for God to remove the stress from your life, and He will.

WALK IN THE LIGHT

The last thing that will help us implement our time-management strategy is what I call "walking in the light." This is the most important factor because it taps into God's way of managing time.

Walking in the light of God describes the supernatural way in which we find enough time to do what we need to do. Becoming single-minded and conserving energy both depend upon our doing something. For example, we must be single-minded to see our plan through, and we must prevent stress from sapping all of our strength and energy. But when we walk in the light, something supernatural happens, giving us time to make our day work. It's as if God multiplies time back to us so we can get things done. It's a very supernatural thing.

Walking in the light is also important because it serves as a connection between time and light. In order to understand how to manage time well using supernatural aid, we need to understand the relationship between time and light.

The Bible tells us that God is light. (1 John 1:5) And on many occasions God refers to Himself as light. But I want to suggest that if we understand the connection between time and light, we will have a head start on supernaturally managing our day, our week, our month, or our year, while getting everything done.

The connection between time and light in modern times was first seen by a physicist named Albert Einstein. Almost everyone has heard of Einstein, but it's interesting to me that he was a Jew. Although he wasn't known for being a devoutly religious person, he did proclaim to be part of the Jewish faith. That tells me God chose to give Einstein a revelation about the connection between time and light for a reason.

What Einstein said about the connection between time and light can be summed up in his two theories of relativity.[1] Without getting too technical, all the current studies of cosmology and astrophysics owe something to Einstein's theories. Nothing the scientific community does today can get away from the concepts that Einstein introduced. His theories are very well established, both mathematically and through experimentation. They have become models rather than theories. Einstein's work proved that light is the only unchangeable constant in the universe. Whereas energy can change, light cannot. Other substances in the universe can change and are changing all the time, but light does not change. Light stays the same.[2]

Einstein said something else important to our study of light and its relationship to time: Light has a quantifiable speed. Light moves at a rate of 186,000 miles per second. Nothing is known to move faster. We do know that the closer an object approaches that speed, the more it stretches or expands, but we don't know of anything that moves faster.[3]

An interesting point that Einstein himself made was that the only thing that could possibly cross the threshold of the speed of light would have to be called "eternity."

Now, look at what the Bible said two thousand years ago. The Lord said, "Every good gift and every perfect gift is from above, and cometh down from the Father of lights, with whom is no variableness, neither shadow of turning" (James 1:17). Isn't it interesting that God, who is light, has no variableness nor shadow of turning? That's just what Einstein predicted. He demonstrated mathematically that light is the only unchange-able constant in the universe, but the Bible told us that same truth two thousand years ago.

God is light; He's the Father of lights. He doesn't vary in His ways, and in Him is never any shadow of turning. God is immutable, unchangeable light. Therefore, Einstein's contention that light is the only unchangeable constant in the universe was right on. The Bible said it first, and Einstein proved it mathematically thousands of years later.

Einstein said that if something were able to accelerate to the threshold of light speed and beyond, he wouldn't know how to describe it except to say it must be eternity. Well, what does the Bible have to say about that? Look at 1 Timothy 6:15-16. God says, "Which in his times he shall show, who is the blessed and only Potentate, the King of kings, and Lord of lords; who only hath immortality, dwelling in the light which no man can approach unto."

The Bible says God dwells in unapproachable light. In other words, nothing can get close to or go beyond God's light. Einstein postulated that life as we know it couldn't cross the threshold of light speed without somehow changing. God gave him a revelation that could be demonstrated as mathematically provable and can be empirically validated to confirm to us truths God revealed two thousand years ago.

When I began to understand some things about light, it really helped me understand God a little better. I used to find it a real challenge to get my mind around certain truths about Him. Of course, no one can truly grasp all that the Lord is. But for example, I found it difficult to imagine God being in all places at all times. I just couldn't understand how God could be omnipresent.

I can remember growing up thinking, *How could God be in my room while at the same time He's on the other side of the world in China?* As God began to reveal Himself to me, He showed me this connection between light and time, and it gave me insight into His omnipresence. That really caused my faith to leap forward.

Let's look more at some of the laws of physics that will hopefully help your faith increase just as mine did. Let me begin with a brief analogy that reveals just a fraction of God's power.

If you took a rifle that could fire a bullet at the speed of light, firing it directly along the line of the equator, that bullet would circle the globe seven times before you could even release the trigger after your shot. Isn't that amazing? Just think, while you're reading this and thinking about God, He's already had the opportunity to travel around the world at least seven times. That's how God can be everywhere at one time!

There was a scientist at a university in California who designed a mathematical model to help lay people understand the relationship between light and time according to Einstein's theories.[4] As we've already said, Einstein postulated that the faster you travel, accelerating toward the threshold of light speed, the slower time becomes. Moreover, if you could cross that threshold, you would step over into eternity, where God, who is absolute light, dwells.

With this in mind, the scientist from California described the following model. He said that if you launched a rocket carrying astronauts and it moved at 80 percent of the speed of light, traveling away from the earth for 15 days and back to earth for 15 days, maintaining 80 percent light speed, something strange would happen. Inside the rocket, the astronauts would age 30 days—15 days out and 15 days back. But at 80 percent of the speed of light, they would return to people on earth who had aged 60 days. By traveling at 80 percent of the speed of light, the astronauts would have experienced a stretching or slowing down of time as compared to people living on earth.

This scientist then repeated the model using a velocity of 85 percent light speed. Again, the astronauts traveled 15 days out from earth and 15 days back to earth. However, during this second journey, the people on earth had aged 10 years. A mere increase of 5 percent of the speed of light—from 80 percent to 85 percent—caused a slowing of 10 years' time for the traveling astronauts.

Finally, this scientist placed the astronauts on a rocket traveling at the threshold of light speed, just as close as one could travel without going beyond. As with the other trips, these astronauts shot out 15 days and came back 15 days. However, they probably didn't recognize anything on earth when they arrived back home because the earth would have aged 30,000 years!

The astronauts aged a total of 30 days traveling at the brink of light speed, but time on earth had elapsed 30,000 years. These are mathematically proven models.

Now let's go to the Word where Peter tells us, "One day is with the Lord as a thousand years, and a thousand years as one day" (2 Peter 3:8). This is a remarkable confirmation of the scientific model.

The ratio between 30 days of space travel at the threshold of light speed to 30,000 years of elapsed earth time looks like 30/30,000. Reduce that ratio to 1/1000, and you get a perfect confirmation of Scripture. One day is as 1000 years both scientifically and biblically.

Now, how does that apply to our study of time management? The closer you get to the light, the slower time elapses. Therefore, the more you walk supernaturally in the light of God, the greater capacity you have to get everything done. Time slows down for you. Everyone else is going about their day at normal speed, but for those who are walking in the light, time slows to the point where you're getting things done more efficiently than everyone else. You're on a different schedule; you're on God's time.

Of course, physically it's impossible for us to travel at the threshold of light speed. But spiritually we have the capacity to approach it. Remember, we're spirit-beings living in physical bodies. And spiritually we can do what the Bible calls walking in the light. (John 12:35,36) So, as we walk in the light, we get closer to God until time begins to stretch and we accomplish more. Time is slowed for us. It goes further and lasts longer. So, we can get more things done supernaturally than we could before.

The truth about the supernatural is that it's simply God coming together with man. You are not just a man or woman, you're a temple of the Holy Spirit. You and God have been joined by virtue of the blood of Jesus.

Man brings the "natural" part of the supernatural, and God brings the "super" part. Each has a role to play. Man does the natural part he's assigned to, and then God performs the rest. After man does everything in the natural he knows to do, it's up to God to do the rest. The supernatural will carry anyone over any obstacle that the natural portion isn't sufficient to meet.

People sometimes say to me, "Boy, I can't really take time today to spend an hour or two with the Lord. I've got a wild schedule, and I've got to get started early. I just can't take as much time to be with the Lord today."

I know how they feel. Sometimes I feel the same way, but when I make myself spend time with the Lord anyway, tapping into the supernatural, somehow my day works out better. Everything fits into my schedule, and everything gets done. Now I know why. The more I walk in the light, the more time supernaturally slows down for me. I'm able to do more and get more done when I first spend time with the Lord.

Do you remember what happened to Enoch? He certainly practiced walking in the light. He got so close to God that he walked across that threshold of light into the direct presence of God! Just as Einstein postulated, Enoch ceased to exist on this earth as we know it. He crossed over to eternity. (Genesis 5:24; Hebrews 11:5)

That should be an inspiration to us. We can walk with God in a way that stretches time so we've got more than enough of it to do everything God has called us to do. There's no sense in being overwhelmed by trying to get our schedule finished in our own strength.

Since God is light and God and His Word are one, we can begin walking in the light by getting into the Word of God.

Prayer will also bring us into the presence of God. So walking in the light is not only reading and studying the Word, it's also praying and communing with God.

But remember, don't leave God at your prayer closet door when you leave for work. Be occupied with God throughout your day, everywhere you go, communing with and talking to Him from your heart.

Practice being consciously aware of the presence of God as you talk to others. Include God in your thoughts when you're dealing with a problem or a negative circumstance.

Don't occupy your thoughts with your bankers or your creditors to the exclusion of God. Be conscious and aware of God every moment of your day. That's walking in the light.

Practicing these principles will help you master your time and implement your time-management strategy. You must learn to be single-minded, and you must conserve your energy, preventing stress and anxiety from sapping all your strength. And, most importantly, walk in the light. Once you do this, you're on your way to being a master manager of your time.

Remember, God will help you.

SEVEN

RESOURCE MANAGEMENT

Simplifying our lives is a skill we all need to cultivate. We're all called to become better managers, stewards, or administrators for the most high God.

As I have pointed out before, all those resources can be categorized into three groups—time, material things (money), and relationships.

If we look across the body of Christ today, we'll see that few things tend to complicate the lives of believers more consistently and completely than money.

Complications resulting from the mismanagement of money tend to spill over into our relationships as well. That's why a high percentage of divorces in this country cite financial issues as a key factor.

Contrary to popular religious belief, God isn't against our having wealth. God wants us to have abundant material resources. He delights in blessing His children. The problems with money arise when we mismanage this important resource.

Financial resources can be thought of in different terms. For example, money is certainly a financial resource, but so are possessions and property. However, for the sake of simplicity, we will refer to money in general as being one's financial resources.

The money we acquire is something we have a mandate to manage as God's stewards. So, we're really managing money on God's behalf. He put all the resources on this earth and they are His to begin with, so we're just being stewards over His possessions.

God has a lot to say about money. Actually, He says more about money and our relationship to it than any other single subject in the Bible. For example, out of the thirty-eight parables Jesus taught, sixteen have something to say about money. In the New Testament alone, there are five hundred verses that cover both prayer and faith, but a whopping two thousand that deal with money. It's obviously an important subject to God and something we should be knowledgeable about.

DEFINE YOUR OBJECTIVE

One of the most important steps we can take when it comes to money management is to set an objective or a goal. We must know where we're going with our finances. If we're going to develop a plan, we need to set a goal or define our objective to see that our plan comes to pass. Our objective should line up with God's objectives; otherwise, He's not going to be involved in our plan. He won't empower us financially to pursue our own agenda or unbridled self-interest.

Ask yourself, *What is my objective in financial planning?* Now think about that for a moment, and be honest with yourself. Is your objective for making money a retirement home? Is it to generate a sizable savings account so you can semi-retire, taking a little vacation here and there? Is it to send your kids through college? Buy a new car? Get out of debt? These are all good things, but some things are more needful than others.

Saving money for retirement, vacations, or personal purchases are good and necessary things. We should do these things with our money, but we should also add to them the goal of planting seed into God's kingdom. Sowing seed into the kingdom of God must be our final objective, our motive for managing our money.

Now some of you might be thinking, *Man, this is radical! Are you telling me I'm working like a dog, trying to make ends meet, so I can give more? Who are you kidding?*

Well, first of all, I'm not telling you anything. God's the One who says we're supposed to give with a priority into His kingdom. Besides, it all comes from God in the first place, so it's not really ours to begin with. So, how hard can it be to give away something that doesn't belong to us? We're just managing it.

God says working with a priority toward giving into His kingdom will bring us the greatest measure of blessing. (Matthew 6:33) We have to embrace this objective as our own. But we can't really do that until we're able to associate our best interests with God's best interests. Unfortunately, many people never do that. They make excuses, saying, "Well, according to the Bible, I've got to work and labor anyway. Now I have to just give it all away?" If they only realized it, giving into God's kingdom *is* in their best interest. My goal is to help you realize that.

The simple truth is that if we will work for God, He will work for us. However, if we work for ourselves only, then we're on our own. And if you know yourself as well as I know myself, that's one place I don't want to be—on my own.

We get confronted with the futility of our own efforts all too often. We need God, and God needs us because we're His body on the earth. We're His hands, His feet, and His voice. We should be able to say, "Okay, God, I'll work for You. I'm going to measure everything I have in this life for its effectiveness in getting more people saved, more people healed, and more people grown up in Your Word. I'm going to labor to manage my finances efficiently, as You say I should, for the sole purpose of being able to plant as much seed into Your kingdom as possible."

You see, when we work for God like that, He'll take care of us. That's what the Bible says. Jesus said this when He gave His famous teaching about seeking first the kingdom of God. He was saying that all the unbelievers in the world just want houses and clothes and food. They get anxious about it and wonder where those things are going to come from. But believers don't have to be worried about such things. Take no thought about it. All we have to do is seek the kingdom of God first, and then we can have all those other things. (Matthew 6:31-33)

We get into trouble when we try to figure out how God brings these things to pass. So often we get worried, thinking, *What if I seek first the kingdom and God doesn't come through?*

How is God going to bring me these things if I don't save up for them by scrimping or borrowing? How will these things be added unto me?

Well, that's not our problem to worry about; that's God's part. His Word clearly tells us not to lean on our own understanding because His ways are higher than ours. (Proverbs 3:5; Isaiah 55:8) If you can figure out how God is going to perform His Word, it probably isn't of God. He could bring your answer in a way you never thought of. It could come through a rich uncle you didn't even know you had. It might be a bonus or an increase in salary. Who knows, it could even come from the profit of a witty idea or invention that makes you money. God may prosper you in a way you might not even be able to imagine.

The important thing for us is to seek first the kingdom of God. It's crucial for us to know exactly what the kingdom of God is. Jesus defines it several places in the New Testament, using parables to describe it. One of the most important parables He uses is found in Mark 4, where He talks about the seed principle. In this passage, Jesus says the kingdom of God is like a man who casts seeds in the ground and afterward goes to sleep. Over the next couple of days that seed springs up and begins to grow, though the man doesn't know how it happens. This, Jesus says, is what the kingdom of God is like. (Mark 4:26,27)

This is the kingdom we're supposed to seek first. We're supposed to seek ways to base our life on the seed principle. It's totally scriptural and accurate to say that our motivation for managing our money is to plant as much seed into the kingdom

of God as we can. We can view this as being God's objective for
us in the area of finances.

CREATE A
SPIRITUAL ATMOSPHERE

It's not enough to create just a one-time prosperity event in
our lives. We must create an atmosphere surrounding us that
enables God to become involved in meeting our needs moment
by moment. This is creating a spiritual atmosphere.

Paul spoke to the Philippian church about this very thing.
He said, "Now ye Philippians know also, that in the beginning
of the gospel, when I departed from Macedonia, no church
communicated with me as concerning giving and receiving,
but ye only" (Philippians 4:15).

The church at Philippi was a very generous church. Paul
even encouraged other churches to become like the Philippians. In the midst of their great poverty, this church was determined to plant every seed conceivably possible into the
kingdom of God.

They didn't have it to give, but they scratched it together
anyway. And in the middle of a trial of great affliction, they
gave with the right attitude. They gave out of a deep joy in their
hearts. Even though they didn't have it naturally, they found a
way to give it because their priority wasn't to meet their own
need—it was to plant seed. And they did so rejoicing.

Notice what Paul told them. He said, "But my God shall
supply all your need according to his riches in glory by Christ

Jesus" (Philippians 4:19). This is one of the most famous Scriptures in the Bible, and it's addressed to the church who created a spiritual atmosphere.

Paul didn't tell them, "God will supply all your need according to your paycheck, or your level of education, or the number of hours you work in a week." No, God supplied all their need according to His riches in glory. There's no limit to that!

But we do have to meet the requirements. We must create the same kind of spiritual atmosphere the Philippian church created. It's not enough to just say, "Yes, brother, I believe in the prosperity message. God shall meet my needs." We must give with the same heart the Philippian church had, and that was to give everything they could possibly give to the preaching of the Word. They didn't do it grudgingly or out of condemnation, but they did it out of the abundance of their joy. They couldn't wait to give. Therefore, it was to these people that God said He'd meet their need according to His riches in glory.

I want you to see that what they actually did was create a spiritual atmosphere in which God could meet their needs. It was an atmosphere pleasing to God. Paul said the following about that atmosphere:

> But I have all, and abound: I am full, having received of
> Epaphroditus the things which were sent from you, an odour of
> a sweet smell, a sacrifice acceptable, wellpleasing to God.
>
> Philippians 4:18

Notice the word *odor* in this verse. The Greek word means "fragrance or of a sweet smelling savor."[1] It refers to an aroma of something pleasing. The Philippians created an atmosphere that was so sweet, so fragrant, and so appealing that it pleased the Lord. Obviously, it wasn't a natural fragrance, it was a spiritual fragrance or atmosphere the Philippians created.

God is saying that when we manage our money to give our best seed into God's kingdom, it will produce a spiritual atmosphere well-pleasing to Him. This, in turn, enables Him to give back His divine provision to us. It's not a matter of giving some money and then trying to believe with all our might for a thirty-, sixty- or hundred-fold return on that gift. On the contrary, we can create an atmosphere that will produce God's provision every moment and every second of every day. We can walk in a spiritual atmosphere that is sweet and well-pleasing to God all the time. Think about that. We can create a spiritual atmosphere just by our approach to money and with the goal in mind of giving as much as possible into His kingdom. Of course, it's impossible to please God without faith, so this kind of giving must be done in faith. But when we give first to God out of a heart to increase His kingdom, we create a spiritual atmosphere that allows Him to multiply blessings back to us.

He will increase us with every good thing—His peace and His joy, as well as financial increase. And we can walk in this kind of climate, this kind of atmosphere, every minute of every day. God's involvement in meeting our need is an ongoing thing when we adopt this attitude toward money.

In John 12, after Jesus raised Lazarus, He went home and ate with him. Mary and Martha were there, and good ol' Martha was serving again.

At some point, Mary took a pound of spikenard ointment, a very costly oil, and anointed Jesus' feet with it. Afterward, the entire house was filled with the fragrant odor. There's that word again—*odor*. It's the spiritual atmosphere of sacrifice we're talking about.

When Judas Iscariot saw this happening, he piped up and began to criticize, saying, "Why was not this ointment sold for three hundred pence, and given to the poor?" (John 12:5). Jesus basically told Judas to keep quiet, and then He said something very important. He said, "Against the day of my burying hath she kept this. For the poor always ye have with you; but me ye have not always" (John 12:7,8).

Now, I could get really sidetracked in this passage, because if you've ever heard people try to link poverty with spirituality, this passage proves them wrong. Have you ever heard religious people say, "Well, Jesus was poor because He said He had no place to lay his head"?

That's not a commentary on the state of Jesus' finances. It's a commentary on the fact that He had a traveling ministry. Jesus didn't have a place to lay his head because He ministered as He traveled from place to place. Jesus wasn't poor, and John 12:7-8 proves it!

He said, "You will always have the poor with you, but not Me." In other words, He places some distance between Himself and the poor. He's the solution for poverty, and therefore, He commended Mary for giving a gift that would help His ministry.

In essence, Jesus commended Mary for managing her money well enough to be able to purchase an ointment that costly. Just imagine if Mary hadn't been good at resource management! She couldn't have given her best gift to the kingdom of God.

It was a precious oil that Mary used to anoint Jesus' feet. At that time, three hundred pence was a year's wages for the average man. She probably had to save up for a long time in order to purchase such a costly ointment. This indicates that she was good at managing her money and planning for the future. She gave her best, that which cost her something, to anoint Jesus' feet.

Notice also that it was Jesus' feet Mary anointed and not His head or some other part of His body. You see, in the New Testament, feet are always associated with somebody who was preaching the Gospel.

For example, the Bible says that the feet of believers are to be shod with the preparation of the Gospel of peace. (Ephesians 6:15) In other words, a believer should be prompted and motivated to go out and preach the Gospel to all the world. The Bible describes the feet of those who preach good news as being beautiful. (Isaiah 52:7)

By anointing Jesus' feet, Mary provided an example as to how believers should use whatever precious resource they have available to undergird and support the preaching of the Gospel.

Unfortunately, it seems as if there's always somebody, usually sitting in the peanut gallery, who wants to criticize what some preacher has been given. On occasion, someone will pipe up and say something like, "Hey, that ought to be used for the poor."

After a convention one time, somebody stood up and said something negative about a Rolex watch the preacher was wearing. He said, "You ought to sell that watch and give it to the poor." Well, that's the kind of thing Judas said.

Of course, that critical person had no idea how many watches the preacher had given away in the past. Or, for that matter, he had no idea who gave the watch to this preacher in the first place. This person was just being critical.

It's never right to criticize what somebody gives in support of the preaching of the Gospel. Those who do, align themselves with the spirit of Judas, the spirit of a thief. Judas wasn't truly concerned about the poor, he was jealous that somebody else had something he didn't have. That's why Jesus rebuked him.

God takes care of His ministers. What God gives to someone is sacred and not to be criticized. When His people create a pleasing spiritual atmosphere toward God, God will see to it they are blessed. Jesus commended Mary for her giving, and it was pleasing to Him because it contained the aroma of sacrifice.

Think about right now what a fragrant aroma smells like. What happens when you come into a room and get hit with a blast of citrus or vanilla fragrance? It gets your attention, doesn't it? It's pleasant to smell. You tend to follow that aroma and look for its source.

That's exactly how God responds to our fragrance of sacrifice when we give to Him our best. He takes notice; it pleases Him. God gravitates toward that kind of a spiritual atmosphere, and He responds to it. He's pleased with the fragrance of our giving when it's the best. The more precious the fragrance, the more God is pleased with it, because it takes faith to give with that kind of a heart toward God, and we know that God is pleased by faith.

The more faith we have, the more God is pleased.

DESIRE TO GIVE THE BEST

From time to time people have approached me and said, "Hey, I really don't have this kind of desire to please God the way you're talking about."

Usually, these people *want* this desire, but they just don't have it. I tell them that the goal of managing their money should be to give the best they have into God's kingdom, but honestly, sometimes it's not really their primary goal, and it makes them feel guilty or condemned. That's not a good feeling. They know their desire should be to give as much as possible to God, but usually other interests have come first. For example, they may want to pay off some debt first or take a relaxing vacation.

How do you change your desire when it comes to something like this? The Bible says, "Lay not up for yourselves treasures upon earth, where moth and rust doth corrupt, and where thieves break through and steal" (Matthew 6:19). Stashing away things for yourself only is called selfishness. It would be in your best interest to give first into the kingdom of God. And here's the reason why:

> *But lay up for yourselves treasures in heaven, where neither moth nor rust doth corrupt, and where thieves do not break through nor steal:* for where your treasure is, there will your heart be also.
>
> Matthew 6:20,21

When we lay up or save money for ourselves only, we're investing our desire into those things, because that's where our heart is. But when we give into the kingdom of God, we're not only planting seed into God's kingdom where nothing and no one can corrupt or steal it, we're also creating a heart or a desire for the kingdom of God.

Where we spend our money indicates where our interests truly lie. If you spend a lot of money on golf, people can tell golf is important to you. You wouldn't spend money on golf if it wasn't important to you. The Bible says, "Where your treasure is, there will your heart be also" (Matthew 6:21).

Suppose you invested money in a particular stock in the stock market. Once you did that, you'd be interested in that stock. Although there are thousands of stocks you could be interested in, you're only interested in the one you purchased. You couldn't care less about the others. Your treasure or your heart is in that one stock, because that's the one you invested in. The next thing you know, you can't open a newspaper without checking on your stock. You have created a desire for that stock. It's your treasure.

The same thing is true of the kingdom of God. Once we invest into God's kingdom, we find that we can't wait to see His Word preached. Our heart is in that thing. We can't wait until Sunday morning to find out more about the things of God and where our treasure is. We can't wait to place more treasure into the kingdom, adding to our original investment. We've created a desire for the things of God. Our heart is involved, and we desire to give into it above anything else. Where your treasure is, your heart follows.

USE MONEY TO MAKE FRIENDS

Managing money in a way that gives us the maximum amount to give into God's kingdom will not only create a fragrant spiritual atmosphere pleasing to God, increasing our desire to become interested in God's kingdom, but it will also allow us to make friends.

That last benefit may strike you as odd, but here is what the Word says: "And I say unto you, Make to yourselves friends of the mammon of unrighteousness" (Luke 16:9).

The phrase "mammon of unrighteousness" isn't a commentary on whether or not money is good or bad. There is no inherent goodness or evil in money. It depends on how money is used. God is saying that we should use our money, our mammon of unrighteousness, to make friends.

As believers, we're not supposed to make intimate friendships with unbelievers. Of course, we are to be polite and friendly, but we should avoid choosing non-Christians to be our counselors or confidants. The reason being that the Bible says, "Be ye not unequally yoked together with unbelievers: for what fellowship hath righteousness with unrighteousness? and what communion hath light with darkness" (2 Corinthians 6:14). The obvious answer is none.

When the Bible tells us to use our money to make friends, it's talking about using our money to get people saved. That's the plain and simple truth.

So, we are to make friends with the mammon of unrighteousness to get people saved but also to receive an eternal reward. Now let's look at the entire verse.

> And I say unto you, Make to yourselves friends of the mammon of unrighteousness; that, when ye fail, they may receive you into everlasting habitations.
>
> Luke 16:9

The word *fail* in this context means "to die." When you die and go home to be with the Lord, "they," meaning the people who have gotten saved because you used your money the right way, will receive you into everlasting habitations.

The Bible talks about a glorious home going or an abundant entrance into heaven. One of the things that I think will make it such an abundant entrance is this special reception.

We have no idea how many people are affected by the proper use of our money. There are certain ministers who preach to hundreds of thousands of people, getting sinners saved and filled with the Holy Spirit all the time. When we help support such ministers, we are partaking in their reward. When the time comes, all those people who enter into the kingdom because we used our money for the Gospel will be lining the roadways of heaven to welcome us into an everlasting habitation.

FAITHFUL IN LITTLE

Being faithful with our money is only the first step in faithfulness. We must first exercise faithfulness in the least before we can be entrusted with greater things.

God's Word says, "If therefore ye have not been faithful in the unrighteousness mammon, who will commit to your trust the true riches?" (Luke 16:11). For example, we must learn to be faithful with our money before we could ever be considered faithful to serve in the church as an usher, a greeter, a Bible study leader, or an intercessor.

Wherever a man's treasure is, there his heart will be also. Faithfulness begins by putting treasure into God's kingdom before faithfulness in other areas can truly develop. As stewards or managers on God's behalf, money considerations come first. When we prove we're faithful with that area, God will entrust us with true riches.

God's true riches are not money. Money is the least of God's provisions for us to manage. The Bible defines true riches as the manifold grace of God. Take a look at the following scripture:

As every man hath received the gift, even so minister the
same one to another, as good stewards of the manifold grace of
God.

1 Peter 4:10

Every believer is endowed with spiritual gifts intended by God to be used as a channel for His anointing on the earth. As a believer, you may be endowed with a gift of healing, the working of miracles, or another spiritual gift. This is God's plan for us as His stewards. Ultimately, we are to be managers of the power of God. Isn't that wonderful? That's the true riches of God.

When we can lay our hands on the sick and watch them get healed before our eyes, when we can speak to the dead and see them rise, or when we witness God restore sight to the blind and hearing to the deaf, we are truly rich! How can money compare to these things?

God wants us to be a conduit for the working of miracles and for the anointing of God. He wants His power to flow into the earth through us. But first we have to prove faithful in that which is least in God's kingdom. That means we'll need to be wise managers of our money.

It's in our best interest to become a good steward of our finances. Giving our best into God's kingdom will produce rich rewards.

As we begin to plan a budget for the purpose of sowing as much seed into the kingdom of God as possible, we'll create a desire to see even more accomplished for God. When our objective is to seek the kingdom of God first, we're sure to prosper.

Along the way, of course, we'll create a sweet-smelling, spiritual atmosphere in which God can multiply blessings back to us. As we prove ourselves faithful in the area of financial planning, God will increase our responsibilities. He'll entrust more to us, and we'll graduate to higher responsibilities and the true riches of God.

EIGHT
MANAGING YOUR INCOME

When talking about resource management, we must realize that there are two sides to the same coin. On one side we have income management, and on the other side, we have expense management. Let's look at the side of income management.

The Bible says, "Let him that stole steal no more: but rather let him labour, working with his hands the thing which is good, that he may have to give to him that needeth" (Ephesians 4:28).

In this life, there is something good for you to do, something good to put your hands to. That's consistent with what the Bible says. You possess certain gifts, talents, and abilities that define what is good for you to do for a living. When you labor in that area, you will be the most productive and fulfilled.

If you're working at a job you don't like, remember what the Word says and begin to pray about it. God says He will give you the desires of your heart. (Psalms 37:4) Therefore, if you desire to be doing something else, ask God to show you how to find it, and He'll open the door of opportunity. Believe Him for it, and then get in there and do it. Work diligently and consistently, and God will bless you.

You don't obtain an income by quitting your job and living by faith. That's how you starve to death. God says that financial responsibility begins with diligence and consistency in laboring at that which is good. If you do anything less, you're a thief.

God didn't tell us to stand in a welfare line in order to generate an income. The welfare system is designed to be a blessing to those who encounter a crisis situation. It's not an escape from the responsibility God says is yours. As we embrace this truth and work for that which is good, God will bless us and we'll produce an income.

Once you have an income, you have something to manage. However, there are some intermediate concerns that must be considered first. For example, you and your family have needs which have to be addressed. You don't labor, generate an income, and give everything away to a stranger. You must provide for your family's needs first.

Unfortunately, I see some people doing just the opposite. They either don't know any better, or they hear someone on TV saying he's prophesying to them to clean out their bank account and send him the money, and they do it. Sadly, that happens, even though it shouldn't. You don't labor to obtain an income just so you can give it away to someone claiming he has need of it.

God says that if we don't take care of our own family, we're worse than unbelievers. (1 Timothy 5:8) God doesn't want you or your family to become a burden to society. Think about it. How can you be a light to the world if the world is supporting you? You can't. God tells each of us to labor at that which is good, and we've got a responsibility to do just that. We need to use that income to meet our family's needs.

Once we've done that, then we can move on to meeting the needs of others as we are able and as we feel led.

THE SECRET OF THE TITHE

There's one other subject of importance that comes into play after we've labored and generated an income—it's the secret of the tithe. The tithe is something we have to understand because it's part of God's plan to help bless our life. Tithing is not some legalistic requirement God zapped us with for no good reason. It's also not something we must respond to with no real understanding of how it works. Tithing that way will not benefit us. There is a right way and a wrong way to tithe, and we need to know the difference.

The secret of the tithe is that it's the first step in the money-management process. We talked about creating a spiritual atmosphere by giving our best unto the Lord, and tithing is one of the ways this is done.

To tithe simply means to give the firstfruits of your increase. It literally means "one-tenth."[1] Tithing is giving one-tenth of the firstfruits of increase.

In the Old Testament, where the tithe is talked about most, it's generally put in agricultural terms because it was written to an agricultural society that raised livestock and grew crops as a way of supporting themselves. So, much of the terminology surrounding the subject of the tithe in the Old Testament is worded in crop or livestock terminology and refers to the very best of the livestock or crop.

To our way of thinking, that may sound a little strange, but the agricultural association can be replaced with terms associated with money. Livestock and agricultural products were used as a measurement of wealth in the Old Testament, but in our day, we deal in dollars and cents. Of course, the tenth of all increase remains the same. It still means we are to tithe of our firstfruits, whether it's a herd of cattle or a weekly paycheck.

In our society today, we would tithe the first 10 percent of our income to God.

And one other thing, God doesn't tell us to tithe the first-fruits to Uncle Sam and the secondfruits to Him.

Everything you earn—your entire paycheck before taxes—is called your gross income. Just because some of your paycheck is automatically deducted and sent to Uncle Sam doesn't mean you didn't earn it. You earn the gross, and the firstfruits, or one-tenth, of that go to the Lord.

Many people resist the teaching of the tithe. I don't see how anyone can really do that because the Bible is full of teachings on the subject in both the Old and New Testaments. Nevertheless, there are now more preachers than ever before telling people they don't have to tithe.

It's something that's easy to preach, and people's flesh wants to hear it. I heard a guy preach not too long ago that the tithe was just a form of Old Testament civil taxation. He argued that because Israel was a theocracy, the tithe was the only way they could raise money for municipal projects and such things.

That's ridiculous. If someone is going to use that kind of logic for the tithe, he also has to extend it to the whole Word of God. He would have to say, for example, since Israel was a theocracy, the Ten Commandments was just a form of civil law that could be ignored today as well.

It's important to understand godly principles and how they affect us today. The tithe is not something unique to the Old Testament and not something that's under the Law, either. In fact, the commandment to tithe predates the Law of Moses by over four hundred years. Abraham paid tithes to Melchizedek four hundred years before the Law was given.

However, the principle of the tithe appears even before that. The tithe is first mentioned in the book of Genesis. It's one of the central issues surrounding the fall of man and one of the most significant theological considerations surrounding the tree of the knowledge of good and evil.

We know that Adam was placed in the Garden of Eden as God's steward. He gave Adam dominion over the earth and everything in it, but He didn't give Adam the earth. The earth remained God's. Adam was just there to dress it and keep it. It was a kind of training intended to teach Adam and the rest of us how to be good stewards with a few things until Adam and others could be trusted with many things.

Adam was God's first steward, but he was not God's property owner. Adam had the power of attorney to act on his Lord's behalf as long as his interests represented the Lord's interests.

There's always something that distinguishes the owner from the steward; otherwise, the steward becomes equal to the owner. So to distinguish the steward from the owner, God put the tree of the knowledge of good and evil in the Garden and said, "Don't eat fruit from this tree." (Genesis 2:17) Why did God say that?

It was important for Adam to acknowledge God's sovereignty and authority through the act of obedience. He had his boundaries, and they included not partaking of the tree of the knowledge of good and evil.

When you rent a house, you can do most of the things the owner can do to the house, but there are certain things you can't do. For instance, you can't burn it down or sell it. On the other hand, you can decorate it and fix it up. You can do a lot of things with that house even though you're just renting it. Renting someone else's house gives you *some* rights but not *all* rights to that house.

This is the difference between stewardship and ownership. As the owner of the earth, God told Adam to respect His authority and not eat the fruit from a certain tree. As long as Adam respected God's commandment, he could continue to enjoy dominion over the earth. However, the moment Adam overstepped his right of stewardship, he broke God's commandment and usurped God's authority. In essence, when he bit into the forbidden fruit, he was attempting to elevate himself to God's level, and as a result, he got evicted.

This demonstrates the principle of the tithe. Here and elsewhere in the Old Testament, God told man to respect what was His. God repeatedly set aside things that were not to be touched. He established a distinction between His sovereignty and man's stewardship. He said, "I've given you everything that pertains unto life and godliness." (2 Peter 1:3) "But this one thing you don't touch—the tithe. The tithe belongs to Me." (Numbers 18:26)

When we tithe, we are submitting our interests in the material world to God, giving Him authority in our lives. By our actions, we are recognizing that He is the sovereign owner and we are the stewards. However, if we don't tithe, we're following the same course of rebellion Adam followed when he overstepped his stewardship boundaries. We're tampering with God's property inappropriately.

Satan will encourage us not to pay God our tithes, just as Satan tempted Eve to eat of the forbidden fruit. He can make it sound pretty good too. He might say, "Surely God knows your heart. He knows the financial bind you're in right now, and He will understand if you don't tithe this time. Surely it won't hurt anything if you leave off tithing."

It's a lie! When we listen to Satan and withhold our tithes from God, we usurp His authority just as Adam did. Withholding our tithes is tantamount to disavowing our position as God's steward on the earth, and it will cost us our dominion and our authority as surely as it did Adam. We will lose our authority in the area of our finances if we do not tithe our first-fruits to the Lord.

Sometimes it's difficult as a pastor to tell this to certain people. It goes against my natural thinking, for example, when I have to tell this to a single-parent mom who is really struggling financially, trying to take care of her family. Nevertheless, I'm obligated to tell her, "You need to give God ten cents out of every dollar you earn. It's better for you if you do because it's the only way God can be involved in your financial life."

When a person understands the principle behind the tithe, it's much easier to become a tither. As tithers, we are simply recognizing God's authority in our lives and submitting our interest in this material world to that authority. This is what enables God to entrust us with additional resources to manage on His behalf. This is the beginning of God's blessing in our lives.

If we can't tithe, then God can't trust us with additional resources, because all we'll do is consume them on our own lusts. It's really in our best interest to tithe to prove our dependability in the kingdom of God. Then, as we prove ourselves faithful in the most basic of resources, God will increase our potential to manage more on His behalf.

NEW TESTAMENT TITHING

There are many places in the Word where we can study about the tithe, but I think it will benefit us to see examples of tithing in the New Testament. I hear so many people say,

"Well, tithing is just an Old Testament practice. There's nothing in the New Testament about the tithe."

They must have never read the New Testament, because it has a lot to say about the tithe. Look at the following portion of Scripture: "Wither the forerunner is for us entered, even Jesus, made an high priest for ever after the order of Melchizedek" (Hebrews 6:20).

I'm sure most everybody is familiar with the present-day ministry of Jesus, our High Priest. After He was raised from the dead, Jesus sat down at the right hand of God, where He is today making intercession for us as our High Priest.

I think a lot of people don't know about Jesus' high priestly role and how He associates Himself with the order of Melchizedek. Melchizedek was the priest to whom Abraham gave a tithe in the Old Testament. Not much is known about Melchizedek, because not much is written about him in the Bible. However, Jesus compared His high priestly role to this priest in the Old Testament.

What we do know about Melchizedek is found in the following passage of Scripture:

> For this Melchizedek, king of Salem, priest of the most high God, who met Abraham returning from the slaughter of the kings, and blessed him; to whom also Abraham gave a tenth part of all; first being by interpretation King of righteousness, and after that also King of Salem, which is, King of peace.
>
> Hebrews 7:1,2

That's about as much as the Bible tells us about Melchizedek's ministry. He did two things: He received tithes from Abraham (one-tenth of Abraham's increase), and he blessed Abraham. However, time and time again, especially in the book of Hebrews, Jesus is described as being our High Priest according to the order of Melchizedek.

Let me propose something. Do you suppose the blessing Melchizedek gave Abraham was contingent upon Abraham's recognition of his high priestly ministry? Suppose, for example, Abraham had blown Melchizedek off, withholding his tithe. If this had been the case, Abraham would not have acknowledged Melchizedek's high priestly ministry. But by giving Melchizedek a tenth of the spoils, Abraham showed respect for Melchizedek's role as high priest and received a blessing along with it.

The Hebrew word for "to bless" in this context means "empowered to prosper."[2] When we hear about the blessing of God being on somebody's life, it's the same as God's empowering him or her to prosper. Prosperity isn't measured only in dollars and cents. Prosperity is the measured increase of anything that relates to the life of God. It could be an increase in good health, joy, or peace.

When God says He will bring blessing into our lives, that means He will empower us to experience these kinds of increases. That's what we saw Melchizedek doing for Abraham and that's part of the high priestly ministry of Jesus.

Jesus is now at the right hand of the Father to confer blessings on His children, to empower us to prosper. We are to recognize His ministry as High Priest the same way Abraham recognized Melchizedek—by paying the tithe.

It's completely inappropriate and unscriptural for Christians today to cry out for the blessings of Jesus, our High Priest, when we don't even tithe. How can Jesus function as our mediator, advocate, and intercessor when we haven't even recognized His high priestly ministry? We must recognize it before we can expect the blessing from it.

THE HIGH PRIESTLY ROLE OF JESUS CHRIST

What are the blessings of God, specifically? We talk a lot about how Jesus blesses His people, but do we really know what He does as our High Priest? Let's take a look at what the Word says.

> *By so much was Jesus made a surety of a better testament.*
> *And they truly were many priests, because they were not suffered to*
> *continue by reason of death: But this man, because he continueth*
> *ever, hath an unchangeable priesthood. Wherefore he is able also*
> *to save them to the uttermost that come unto God by him, seeing*
> *he ever liveth to make intercession for them.*
>
> Hebrews 7:22-25

We just read that Jesus is able to save to the uttermost because He lives to make intercession for us. We access this benefit through tithing because tithing unlocks the blessing.

Don't misunderstand me, I'm not saying that tithing will get you into heaven. Going to heaven comes by confessing with your mouth and believing in your heart that Jesus is the Son of God. (Romans 10:9,10) Being saved "to the uttermost" makes reference to the Greek word *sozo* which can be translated other places in the New Testament as God's ability to deliver, to make whole, to heal, to protect, and to preserve.[3]

The word *sozo* embraces the whole concept of redemption and salvation, describing what the blood of Jesus is able to do for us. There is more to salvation than just sliding into heaven by the skin of our teeth. No, Jesus wants to save us to the uttermost, deliver us to the uttermost, provide for us to the uttermost, and heal us to the uttermost.

Jesus lives to do all those things for us as High Priest, but we must first come to Him through His high priestly ministry. If He's going to be our high priestly intercessor, we must tap into that high priestly role after the order of Melchizedek and recognize this ministry by the payment of our tithes.

> But now hath he obtained a more excellent ministry, by how much also he is the mediator of a better covenant, which was established upon better promises.
>
> Hebrews 8:6

God's Word says that Jesus has obtained a "more excellent ministry" as our High Priest. It's a more excellent ministry because it's better than the Levitical priesthood which preceded it. Moreover, it's a better covenant that Jesus has come to fulfill. Jesus mediated this new covenant based on better promises than the previous covenant.

The word *mediator* is an interesting word. *The Amplified Bible* defines it parenthetically to mean "arbiter" or "agent." We could say Jesus is the agent of our new covenant. Glory to God! He's the One who makes the new covenant happen. As an agent, He is the representative of the new covenant in our lives and must be retained. I would suggest the payment of your tithe is the recognition of that agency, enabling Him to go to work for you as mediator and arbiter of the new covenant.

The new covenant is an exciting thing. The Bible says the following about the new covenant:

> *For this is the covenant that I will make with the house of Israel after those days, saith the Lord; I will put my laws into their mind, and write them in their hearts: and I will be to them a God, and they shall be to me a people.*

Hebrews 8:10

God says His people won't have to teach one another His laws because He will teach them Himself. Sadly, I often bump into Christians who say, "God's not real to me. I wish I could see the glory everybody else sees. I wish I knew things about God everybody else says they know about Him."

The new covenant being fully realized in our lives makes Him real to us; it's life changing. He can be as real to us as the person sitting next to us. However, if you are born again and don't see things in your life that you can attribute to God, or if you have to labor to obey God's Word, or if His Word seems to be far away and hard to understand, I suggest you look at your tithing practices. In order for Jesus to be the mediator of this better covenant, we must acknowledge Him as our High Priest and pay our tithes.

I don't want to make this sound like the tithe is the short-cut to everything in the kingdom of God, but it is important. I'm not suggesting that if we merely pay a tithe, everything else will fall into place. That's not necessarily true. But tithing is a foundational principle upon which everything else is built.

We can be tithers and still miss out on the other blessings of God. For example, we can tithe but not pray. If we're tithing for legalistic reasons with no faith behind it, we're not fulfilling God's other commandments and we'll be unbalanced. Conversely, if we don't tithe, we can pray until we're blue in the face and not much will happen.

Look at what else Jesus does as our High Priest:

> *For we have not an high priest which cannot be touched with the feeling of our infirmities; but was in all points tempted like as we are, yet without sin. Let us therefore come boldly unto the throne of grace, that we may obtain mercy, and find grace to help in time of need.*
>
> Hebrews 4:15,16

Jesus has been touched with the sense of our infirmities, enabling Him to be a compassionate High Priest. He's approach-able and can relate to us because He has experienced everything we'll ever experience and more. So we can come boldly into His presence to find mercy, grace, and help in time of need.

We all need the mercy of God, friend, because there are times when we blow it. We all make mistakes. Sometimes we're disobedient, and we certainly don't deserve the blessing of God. But that's when we need God's mercy most. We don't want to risk not getting God's blessing because we haven't properly acknowledged Jesus with our tithes.

Again, tithing is not meant to be a legalistic act in which we feel we must put our last dime in the offering plate so we'll be blessed. God's blessings can't be bought; He doesn't work that way. He will, however, extend His mercy to those of us who don't tithe because He loves us. He will be as merciful to us as He can, but we will severely limit the extent to which He can bless us. Just remember that He does expect us to grow up.

The Bible says, "Wherefore, holy brethren, partakers of the heavenly calling, consider the Apostle and High Priest of our profession, Christ Jesus" (Hebrews 3:1).

One translation of this verse renders the word *profession* as "confession of faith." It's not just any profession. It's your profession or *confession* of faith. The high priestly ministry of Jesus has a lot to do with our confessions of faith. It's important that we don't become weary in confessing God's Word. As soon as the Word drops down into our hearts and becomes a confession of faith, Jesus will bring it to pass. It's one of His high priestly responsibilities to bring to pass His Word.

Usually, the Word of God doesn't start out as a confession of faith in our mouths. The first few times we start confessing the Word, we're just doing it out of obedience to God. At that point, it's probably not faith yet. For example, if you're confessing your healing in the face of a doctor's negative report or a painful symptom and there's a little fear there still, faith hasn't been fully developed yet. However, when you begin confessing the Word according to Romans 10:17, "Faith comes by hearing," you begin to realize how important it is to continue listening to God's Word.

Our belief system is grounded in what we've heard the most. If you've grown up hearing that you're a stupid or incompetent person, you'll end up believing it. You may have an IQ of 130, but if you've heard something to the contrary, you'll believe you're dumb. You believe what you hear the most.

This is why we confess God's Word. As we begin hearing the Word of God, we can then believe what it says about us. We can't control what we hear from others, but we can control what we tell ourselves. So start confessing the Word in the area you need it the most.

If it's healing you need, start confessing, "By His stripes I was healed." (1 Peter 2:24) The first time you say that, it probably isn't any more of a confession of faith than saying you can fly to the moon. But a few days or weeks later, you could say it with faith. Faith comes by hearing, and one day you're going to confess, "By His stripes I was healed," and it's going to drop into your heart. At that point, it becomes a confession of faith, and the High Priest of your confession of faith will bring it to pass, restoring your body, and granting you healing.

But what if you're not a tither? The Bible says Jesus is the High Priest of your confession of faith. That tells me you could confess until you're blue in the face, but if you don't activate

Jesus' high priestly role by tithing, you'll come up short. Even if you confess the Word in faith, Jesus can't perform as your High Priest until you acknowledge His ministry through the giving of the tithe.

Time and time again, we see the blessing of God tied to the concept of the tithe. Yes, God wants to save us to the uttermost, deliver us to the uttermost, provide for us to the uttermost, and protect us to the uttermost. But all of this comes through Jesus' high priestly ministry. Jesus wants God to be real to us. He is the mediator between God and us. He is the agent of a new covenant, and the essence of that covenant is to bring the reality of God to bear in our lives; but it first comes through His high priestly ministry.

I would suggest to you that the principle of the tithe is one of the most fundamentally important considerations to the Christian walk. When struggling people come to me for guidance, I always ask them three basic questions before I even begin to counsel. In this order I ask, "Are you saved? Are you baptized in the Holy Spirit? Do you tithe?" Without these three cornerstones in place, their lives can get off of the path God intended them to follow.

THE SECRET OF TITHING

We've just looked at the ways our obedience to God's command to tithe can unlock His secret blessings for our lives.

In the book of Malachi, God tells us to "Bring ye all the tithes into the storehouse" (Malachi 3:10). This clearly states that we each have a storehouse where we are to bring all our tithes. It's not scriptural to divide up the tithe and send it off to a bunch of different storehouses. God clearly indicates there is one storehouse, or one church, where we are to bring all of our tithes. That's the church God has called you to, and it's also where you receive your spiritual sustenance.

Now, as far as offerings are concerned, God may direct us to give those in other places, but the tithe still goes to the storehouse. For example, if you have an offering to give to a certain minister but you haven't tithed to your local church first, then you should first tithe to your local church then give to the minister. The tithe comes first, and if there's anything left over, it goes wherever God directs you to give it.

When we make a decision to tithe, we stick with it and then prove God by telling Him, "God, it says in Your Word that I can prove You on the tithe, expecting You to open up the windows of heaven and pour out blessings which there isn't room enough to contain." (Malachi 3:11) "I'm going to do this and tithe until it shuts up the devil."

> Prove me now herewith...if I will not open the windows of heaven, and pour you out a blessing, that there shall not be room enough to receive it.
>
> Malachi 3:10,11

Tithing is the secret to having all our needs met, giving something to those in need, and still having enough left for ourselves. Every other area in our lives can come into order once we've become a dedicated tither, proving God on His Word.

He will honor those who honor Him. Tithing has been, and continues to be, one of the most fundamental ways to honor God. When we tithe, we show our obedience to His authority and open ourselves up to His blessings. God blesses those who willingly place themselves under His authority and who follow His precepts. Tithing is just one of the secrets that unlocks the door to a life less complicated yet full of God's blessings.

NINE

Managing Your Expenses

God wants to bless us every way He can, but we have to understand His plan in order to maximize our results. God has a plan for our finances, and it involves tapping into His principles so that we can prosper. He will prosper us as we learn to follow His precepts in managing our money.

In chapter 8, we examined the income side of managing of our resources; now let's look at the expense side. We must be successful at managing both to be a good steward.

The Bible says, "Let him that stole steal no more: but rather let him labour, working with his hands the thing which is good, that he may have to give to him that needeth" (Ephesians 4:28).

Did that verse say, "Let him work so he can retire at age fifty," or "Let him work that he may have enough to buy a new house or a new car"? No, it says, "Let him work so that he can give to those who have needs." That may mean some people need to make major changes in the way they view life. We work so we can provide for those who have needs.

Obviously, there are a lot of needs in the world, so we have to be selective. We meet the fundamental need of unsaved people by giving them Jesus. We meet the fundamental need of saved people by giving them more of the Word so they can grow up and mature in Christ.

God's plan for us as stewards is to labor, give to others, and of course, tithe into His kingdom. Whatever remains after that is outflow or expense allocation. Here we will call it expense management.

Managing our expenses begins with the same process as managing our time, or anything else for that matter. We have to have a plan. We have to take time to sit down and allow the Holy Spirit, who is the Spirit of understanding, to give us the kind of plan that will enable us to manage our expenses supernaturally. Again, we must have a goal or an objective in order to simplify our lives.

There's a special, technical name for a financial plan such as this. It's called a budget.

We can look at it this way: We're working with the Holy Spirit to plan a budget. (I bet you didn't think budgets were very spiritual, but they are!)

Budgets are fully scriptural. They are a written vision for the financial arena of our lives. (Habakkuk 2:2) So, if you didn't expect to be reading about planning a budget, you had better think again. Budgets are very important to us. Understanding what the Bible says about financial planning and budgeting impacts our capacity to manage money effectively.

There are three basic concerns when it comes to the subject of expense management or budget planning. First of all, we must consider our family's needs. After we've earned an income and tithed, we take care of our family's needs first. Next, we consider debt service, and finally, we plan for debt elimination.

CARING FOR THE
NEEDS OF YOUR FAMILY

Planning for the needs of our families first is scriptural. Again, let's read what the Bible says: "But if any provide not for his own, and specially for those of his own house, he hath denied the faith, and is worse than an infidel" (1 Timothy 5:8).

This is a strong statement, isn't it? Clearly, God expects us to provide for our own, especially those of our own household. But that makes sense. How are we going to be a light to the world and minister to our community if we can't even take care of our own families? If we become social burdens, how in the world are we ever going to minister to other families?

So our first concern after generating an income and giving God what belongs to Him is to take care of our own family needs.

Sadly, I see people missing it in this area all the time. I've heard of some people who find themselves in a financial bind, desperately saying, "Okay, God, I'm going to clean out my bank account and give it all to You. After all, God, You say, 'Give and it'll be given unto you.' You say, 'If you sow bountifully, you'll reap bountifully.'"

So they clean out their bank accounts, which contain all their grocery money, their house payment, and money for their bills, and they just give it away, presumptively expecting God to come through. It can be a cop-out, depending on God to bail them out of a bind they probably got themselves into in the first place. That's not faith; that's presumption.

God expects us to manage our money, taking care of our family's needs first and foremost. Sacrificial giving is something people often misunderstand. Some people will hear an evangelist encouraging them to dig deeper and give sacrificially to his ministry, but unless they've taken care of their basic familial needs and then heard from God regarding what He wants them to give, it's not the appropriate time to give.

The only basis we see in the Word for sacrificial giving relates to a *rhema* word from God. We see an example of this when God sent Elijah to the widow's house. On this occasion, Elijah knocked on her door, saying, "Give me your last morsel of food." (1 Kings 17:13) That was true sacrificial giving. She needed that food for her own survival. However, when she gave to Elijah on God's behalf, she got the miracle she needed.

Sacrificial giving such as this only occurs on rare occasions when God specifically tells us to do something like that. Usually, it's because something dramatic has happened in our lives and we're in desperate need. If that occurs, God will send someone to confirm to you that you are to give that way.

Short of a *rhema* word from God, our regular method of financial management should not incorporate this kind of giving.

DETERMINING NEED

How do we determine need? Sometimes we have a way of kidding ourselves about what a "need" really is. It's useless, however, to try to kid God. He knows what our needs truly are.

Needs are something that can be very subjective. Nobody else can define your need for you, and likewise, you shouldn't stick your nose into somebody else's business attempting to define his or her need either. It bothers me to hear people say, "Look at how extravagant he is with his money." I wish these people would just keep their noses in their own affairs.

Nobody can define what constitutes "need" for another person. It's strictly between that person and God.

Although we share basic needs with everyone, God says that our needs are unique to us, depending on the call of God on our lives, among other things. Each of us has different responsibilities for which we give an account to God.

You're going to need more if you have five kids and two dogs than if you're single. Your responsibilities increase the more people you have to provide for. Your level of need changes. Don't get involved in trying to identify somebody else's need, and don't let them try to influence you in defining what your need should be. You settle that with the Holy Spirit.

It is important to identify our own needs accurately. We need to be sure we are managing our money the way God would have us manage it, so He can bless us. To do this, we need to make sure we're not inflating our need in order to acquire things that aren't really important.

One way to do this is to be sure that we have something set aside to give as seed into the kingdom of God after we've taken care of our family's needs. The Bible promises that if we labor at that which is good and tithe, managing our money correctly, we'll have seed left over. (Ephesians 4:28)

If our financial-management strategy doesn't leave us with anything left over that we can sow as seed, then we're calling something a need that really is not a need.

We are to manage our money in such a way that we'll have something left over for sowing seed.

Here's another way to determine need: "But as God hath distributed to every man, as the Lord hath called every one, so let him walk. And so ordain I in all churches" (1 Corinthians 7:17).

Paul says that the place where we are called and separated unto God is the level at which we are responsible for our financial condition. We're responsible to walk in the light we have.

When you were saved, you were at a certain standard of living that defined your level of need.

Let me give you an example of what I'm talking about. When someone gets saved and God enters his life with an explosion of revelation and excitement for godliness, that's not the time to pretend he's something he's not. The financial condition that existed when that person got saved is the *beginning point* from which he should grow and trust God in the area of finances.

It's like the parable of the talents in Matthew 25 when the master went away on a journey and he gave resources to those he left behind. In this case, he gave money according to each servant's ability to manage it.

Now, in our case, when we were saved, God gave us as many resources as we could be responsible to manage at that time. That point defined our level of need. Then, as the light of God's Word began to increase in us, we began to grow and become responsible for more.

But often when a person gets saved and begins to get ahold of the prosperity message, he mistakenly thinks he can go out and spend beyond his means. I hear about people all the time who go out and buy a big house and a new car after hearing one preacher's prosperity message. They say something like, "Bless God! He wants to prosper me, so I bought this house and car by faith." Well, not really. They're mismanaging their money. They're behaving like unfaithful stewards, and they've complicated their lives immensely as a result.

The same is true on the other end of the spectrum. I've seen those who are rich get saved and hear they should give to those less fortunate. So they give away all they have. Well, that's just as foolish.

Our standard of living at the time we got saved is the starting point, our basic level of need, and it shouldn't be anything else for a while.

Now, if we do things God's way, we won't remain at that level. God is a God of increase, and prosperity is a progressive event. It doesn't happen overnight, but with a little faithfulness, it will happen.

God's Word says that as a steward, a man must be found faithful. (1 Corinthians 4:2) That means we must take that which God has entrusted to us at the outset and be found diligent to manage our expenses within our means. Do it God's way and be faithful. Faithfulness in turn will result in promotion and increase. Don't be overly ambitious and try to be something before you're ready. Rather, work with God on the level at which you were called. God will work with you while you grow and bring increase as you remain faithful.

ELIMINATE YOUR DEBT

Working with God is very important, because He'll help us avoid trouble areas and keep us from falling into such pitfalls as debt.

Debt management is a relevant subject for the body of Christ today, because most Christians struggle with it at some point in their lifetime.

The Bible says, "Owe no man any thing, but to love one another: for he that loveth another hath fulfilled the law" (Romans 13:8). Many people hear that and think that it's a sin to borrow money. In fact, I hear that being preached sometimes, and it grieves my heart because it's a misunderstanding of this verse. It's not unscriptural or sinful to borrow money, and I'll tell you why.

The word translated as *owe* in Romans 13:8 relates to failing to pay or meet an obligation or duty. If you look up the words "to owe" in a concordance, you'll find that it confirms what Scripture says—to owe is to fail to meet an obligation of debt.[1] Therefore, scriptural debt only occurs when you fail to meet an obligation to repay what you've borrowed.

It's not wrong for Christians to borrow money. It's only wrong when Christians don't pay it back. If it were wrong to borrow, God would tell us not to lend. But God says it's okay to lend as long as usurious interest isn't being charged. (Deuteronomy 23:19) In fact, the Bible declares that a sign of covenant blessing is, *We will lend and not borrow.* (Deuteronomy 15:6)

God wouldn't be predicting that we would be lenders if it were a sin to borrow.

I view borrowing money the same way I view the subject of healing. In regard to healing, doctors and medicine aren't bad things. It's not wrong to go to a doctor. The Lord's best may be that you don't have to go to a doctor or use medicine, but using them is certainly not wrong or sinful.

It all has to do with our faith level. Obtaining healing by faith is a progressive process like getting out of debt. Just as most people don't get born again and become immediately filled with divine health, most people don't get born again and immediately pay off their house mortgage. It's a process that gets easier as faith increases.

It's not God's best for us to borrow money, but with moderation, it's certainly not wrong. We will be in a subservient position to our lender when we do borrow; therefore, borrowing needs to be done with caution and prudence. If you can, borrow from a brother or a Christian institution that shares the same value system you do. If you must borrow from a secular institution, be sure you don't engage in an agreement that's contrary to godly principles.

For example, some financial institutions require a cosigner. They'll want a guarantee from somebody, but that's contrary to the Word of God. The Bible warns against the practice of cosigning for another person. (Proverbs 11:15; 17:18) So that's a principle in the Word we have to acknowledge. If you want to borrow money, but the only way you can do it is to get somebody to cosign, then you better be careful not to cross the principles of God's Word. Don't be pressured into doing something you shouldn't.

Nevertheless, if you've already entered into an agreement that required a cosigner, be sure to abide by the conditions of that agreement until the loan is paid off. If you fail to meet those conditions and default on your payment, you're getting into what's called scriptural debt, and that's no place to be.

Remember, it's not wrong to borrow money as long as you can afford to pay it back. So, if you have peace about borrowing for a new house, then go get your mortgage and praise God. But keep listening to the Word and believing God for the speedy payment of that loan. Pretty soon your faith will grow, and the day will come when you'll have your house mortgage paid off and you'll start buying your cars without borrowing any money. You'll be completely out of debt.

So, approach loans cautiously. Ask yourself, "Is this what I need to do right now? Do I have the faith for this project, or do I need help?" If you need financial help, ask yourself, "Can I budget the payments to fit within my current level of income? If I borrow this money, can I still address my family's needs? Is this where my faith is right now?" If you can answer yes to these questions, then get yourself a loan. It beats living in a tent for five years until you get enough faith to buy a house without a mortgage. Go ahead and do it, but don't forget that one of your goals in financial management should be to eliminate your debt completely.

It's good to be out of debt. When we're not encumbered with debt, we have that much more seed to sow into the kingdom of God. There's that much more potential for increase.

Debt elimination occurs only one way, and that's by managing our expenses so that we get seed in the ground of God's kingdom. When we do this, God can supernaturally increase our seed and prosper us richly. Prosperity and increase in life will only come when we do things God's way.

DEBT MANAGEMENT

A budget is used to manage debt so that it can be eliminated. Each family's income level is different, and even that will change over time, but by using some percentages, this is what a typical budget might look like.

First of all, look at your total gross income. This is the combined income of you and your spouse. Typically, most households will have a double income. After you have determined your combined family income, you can start breaking down the numbers. I have a sample of what that might look like for the average family household. But remember, this is a guideline only, not a legalistic sort of document that you have to follow to a tee.

Begin with your gross family income and take 10 percent right off the top for God. Your tithe is important, and God must come first in your financial life. After God comes the IRS. They will take out their percentage whether you ask them to or not.

The amount you're left with is called your disposable income. This is the amount of money you will need to budget in order to manage your household expenses.

First of all, you can't spend more than 100 percent of your income. That should be a no-brainer, but we deal with people all the time who have no idea what their expenses are compared to their income. Consequently, their expenses are consistently anywhere from 20, 50, or even 100 percent more than they earn.

You cannot do that and be a faithful steward according to 1 Corinthians 4. It's your responsibility to manage your expenses within your level of income. Only when you do that will you qualify for promotion and increase.

Realistically, your mortgage will take up about 45 percent of your disposable income. However, with all the taxes, insurance, and utility costs, you may want to allocate more like 50 or 55 percent toward your house payment if you can afford it.

If you decide to do this, you'll end up taking 5 or 10 percent away from something else.

Next is the car payment. That usually requires 15 percent of your disposable income, depending on whether your car or cars are used or new. Insurance and warranties need to factor into that as well. Another 15 percent needs to come out for food, which means you may not be able to eat steak two or three times a week, and you probably won't be able to take the family out to dinner two or three nights a week, either.

It's fascinating to me that when I go into grocery stores, I find the cheapest things to buy are the things that are good for me. The things that are bad for me—ice cream, bakery items, crackers, chips, and soda—are all expensive compared to things like fruits and vegetables. If we eat what's good for us, we'll not only be able to buy more, but also feed our family more nutritionally.

As for the other number breakdowns, I allotted 4 percent for clothing. Now, that's 4 percent according to a man's budget. When my wife saw that only 4 percent was going toward clothes, she about fainted, immediately declaring me a heretic! She said, "Four percent for clothing? Impossible!"

The amount allotted for clothing is one thing that I acknowledge must be measured according to the call of God on your life. For example, if God's got you in a highly visible position where people are constantly measuring and evaluating you according to your appearance, then you need to spend more money for clothes.

My allocation for clothing is more than 4 percent, and that's not just because I'm married to my wife. It is important to me to look nice, and I think it's consistent with the will of God for my life.

After clothing, allot about 3 percent for other debt, including insurance costs such as medical and dental coverage. It's important that you have insurance. It's not fair or appropriate for you to risk your family's financial welfare on how strong a man or woman of faith you are. You can't just say, "I don't need any insurance. I'm not going to get sick or disabled. That's unbelief! I'm not going to die; God's promised me long life."

Yes, He has! If we were all at the stage of perfection where we no longer made mistakes, thereby opening the door to Satan, we would never need insurance. It's a matter of being responsible, providing for our own, and acknowledging our fallibility.

You should love your family enough to have life insurance and plans for funeral expenses. I'm not suggesting that you go out and buy a huge life insurance policy when your funds are tight, but consider the cheapest term insurance you can find and buy that. Be sure you have mortgage cancellation insurance. Purchase something as inexpensive as possible until your increase has come, then you can afford a little more and provide some basic assurances for your family. Part of being responsible is providing for your own.

After insurance, the next three categories of importance are savings, recreation, and miscellaneous. I encourage everyone to take savings seriously. It's important that we discipline ourselves to save money.

I'm not suggesting you save money for a rainy day—that's how you get rainy days. But sooner or later a project will come along, whether it's the kid's college education fund or some future need, and you will want to start making provision for it now. There are some needs we must address today, and there are some needs we must look at down the road. Begin planning for those now. Saving is a good discipline, and it gives us padding if there is an unexpected contingency.

Another area that is often overlooked is recreation. We need to have money set aside for recreation. I don't care how tight your budget is, you need to bring your kids up with the idea that life is fun and enjoyable—not just a drudgery in which you try to make it from one day to the next.

You don't have to do expensive things, but they should be fun. Put some thought into it, and get creative. For example, it doesn't cost much of anything to go camping, fishing, or hiking in the woods, and it's a lot of fun.

Experiences like these can bring you closer together as a family, and that's worth its weight in gold.

The last item to budget is the miscellaneous category. Invariably, unforeseen things pop up that require money. Just like we can't schedule our time right to the minute, we can't schedule our money right to the dollar either. Unexpected contingencies do come up. So, it's necessary to add money to the miscellaneous fund from week to week just in case we need to use it. Unexpected needs do arise, so be prepared for them.

Living within a budget doesn't have to be a lifelong condition. If you do it now, God will promote you and financial increase will come. Be absolutely determined to follow a plan, and God will reward you.

MANAGING CREDIT CARD DEBT

It's impossible to talk about debt management without saying something about credit card debt. Credit card debt is a real problem for many people in our society today. If I had my way, I'd cut up those credit cards and burn them, flush them, or do whatever it took to get rid of them. I counsel more people in financial difficulty because of credit card misuse than any other single factor.

I realize that I can get into a rut on this subject. One day I decided to cut up all my credit cards. However, I soon found out I couldn't check into a hotel without one. So I ended up getting another credit card to use when I travel.

Owning a credit card is not wrong, but misusing it is. If you can't discipline yourself to use credit cards properly, you should cut them up. Otherwise, they're useful for reserving hotel rooms and renting cars; in fact, most car companies won't rent you a car without one.

If you do use a credit card, use it as sparingly as possible and always pay it off the first day you get the bill. It's not smart to pay 18 percent interest per year on credit card debt. At any rate, if you do have a lot of credit card debt, you need to get God involved in your finances so that you can start paying it off.

That brings us to the last item on our sample budget. Set aside about 3 percent of your disposable income for something I call giving to the Lord. This is giving that goes above and beyond the tithe. Use it to put some seed into God's good ground.

It's important that we always protect the 3 percent of our income as giving unto the Lord. Three percent is just an average. When God begins prospering you, the percentage will go up from 3 percent to 10 percent and 20 percent or 50 percent as God gives the increase.

As you begin to prosper financially, start paying off greater amounts of debt. One thing that you may find helpful is to call your creditors and talk to them. Most people don't talk to their creditors because they don't know they should. Try calling your credit card company and telling them you're interested in paying off your debt.

Also tell them if you can't make a payment or if you can only make a partial payment. Let them know you're going to pay something every week or every time you receive a paycheck. Call them regularly.

As a matter of fact, I'd advise you to call them so often, they tell you to stop calling. Use a little reverse psychology, seriously. Call them every week and say, "How are you doing? I'm just reporting in to you that I'm sending you another dollar." Tell them you're interested in paying the principal off instead of just the interest. Ask if they will lower your interest rate. What have you got to lose? Credit card companies will sometimes give breaks on interest rates, but first you have to ask.

Your creditors don't want you to go bankrupt any more than you do. They get nothing if that happens. So, if they know you're trying to make payments, they'll work with you.

Talk to them in a responsible way, assuring them that you're working toward the complete payment of that obligation. They'll love it. They don't want to lose money.

THE BIG THREE BUDGET BUSTERS

It wouldn't be fair to cover debt reduction without going over something I call "budget busters." Budget busters are usually hidden things that prevent us from sticking to our budgets.

The first budget buster is poor record keeping. I encounter people all the time who have no idea how much their utility payments have averaged over the last few months. Likewise, they have no idea how much they really need to allocate for auto maintenance because they didn't keep good records from previous repairs.

With the advent of high-tech computers and simple financial programs, we can make this job even easier. But whether we do it longhand or with the help of a computer program, we all should keep records of our spending habits.

Another budget buster is hidden expenses. Hidden expenses can bust a budget by causing you to spend more than you otherwise would. Let's say you get a little overly optimistic in your expense projections for your car. You think to yourself, *Well, this car is usually very reliable, and I haven't spent much for maintenance in years. I won't need to set aside anything for maintenance now either.* Oh! What a budget buster that is!

If you're going to err, err on the side of being overly liberal rather than too conservative. Set aside a little something extra so unexpected expenses don't eat up your budget.

The third budget buster is probably the biggest and most important of all—impulse buying. Impulse buying will get you every time. When you go grocery shopping, take a list. If you follow that list, you'll know that you're shopping within your budget.

Another tip is to eat before you go grocery shopping. So often we go to the store when we're hungry, and we want to buy everything we see. All the food in the store looks good, and we buy two carts full of groceries on impulse. That's a sure budget buster.

When tempted to buy items not within your budget, try waiting a day or two, and if you still feel like you need it, then make the purchase. If at all possible, don't make purchases on impulse.

Follow a budget and be strict at first as need be. Later, you can relax as God prospers you, and He *will* prosper you if you're faithful. God honors His faithful servants, and He will honor you as you follow His principles and adhere to a good plan for managing your expenses.

There's nothing more liberating than being free of debt. It's a place we should all strive to be. Believe God for it, and He will help bring it to pass. Understand that it's the seed principle that will get you out of debt as you listen to God and follow your budget to financial freedom.

MANAGING YOUR SEED

We've looked at some of God's basic requirements for managing money His way. We've seen how to simplify our finances by becoming better money managers. We pointed out the need to create a spiritual atmosphere in which God is pleased with our giving. We talked about the tithe and the necessity to give to God what is rightfully His. We also looked at how to generate an income and properly manage our expenses. But there's one more very important component involved in the study of resource management. It's something I call "managing your seed."

This is the final and vitally important step in learning to properly manage your resources God's way. Even though we generate income by laboring at that which is good, tithing according to the Word, and properly managing our expenses with a budget, we must still become involved in God's supernatural plan for financial increase if we are going to simplify our lives in line with God's Word.

Tapping into God's increase is eternally linked to the seed principle. This principle is promoted from the beginning of the Bible to the end. For example, God said that seedtime and harvest, along with day and night, will never cease as long as the earth exists. (Genesis 8:22) It is a fundamental principle governing the experience of life on this earth.

If we are going to properly manage our seed by aligning ourselves with God's principles of sowing and reaping, it is vital we understand what the seed is and where it is sown. There's one place the Bible clearly answers these questions, and that's in the parable of the sower. This parable is probably the most important one Jesus ever gave to the body of Christ, because He said that if we understood this parable, we would have the framework for understanding all other parables. (Mark 4:13) In fact, everything Jesus taught is based on the principle of sowing and reaping.

According to the parable of the sower, "the ground" in which the seed is planted is the human heart and "the seed" is the Word of God. Thus, we plant "spiritual seeds" by sharing Jesus and the Word of God with others.

IS MONEY SEED?

Many people misunderstand what "the seed" is all about. Some people talk about money as if it were the seed. Well, technically, that's incorrect. People can't plant a dollar bill into the human heart, but they can use a dollar to plant the Word into the human heart because the Word is "the seed." God's principles and concepts are "the seeds"; the reality of God as seen in the Bible is "the seed."

The Bible does speak of money as seed, when money is used to support the preaching of the Gospel. When the Bible says, "He that ministered seed to the sower" (2 Corinthians 9:10), the Greek word for *seed* in this verse is *sperma;* and in this case, the subject is money.

This portion of Scripture was originally written to encourage the church at Corinth to give support to the church at Jerusalem, because the Jerusalem saints were going through a really difficult time of persecution. God used seed terminology to instruct His people to give money to the believers in Jerusalem.

He is comparing seed to financial giving. When we give money toward the support of the preaching of the Gospel, we're promoting the spiritual growth of our financial seed. In other words, as people hear the Gospel preached, our giving into the kingdom of God can help transform the spiritual condition of these people across the world.

THE SEED MULTIPLICATION PROCESS

As we sow seed, either by sharing the Word or by giving money so others can share, it's good to remember that God says He'll meet our needs. (2 Corinthians 9:9,10) He'll supply bread for our food, He'll multiply the seed we've sown to meet our needs and He'll give us more seed to sow into His kingdom. Our seed is our source of increase. Our seed is our source of prosperity, and that will simplify life. Prosperity doesn't come to us by hoarding what we have been given. Increase in the kingdom of God comes as a result of giving.

God will multiply the seed you've *sown*. When you plant a seed of corn, you don't get a stalk with only one ear of corn on it that has only one kernel of corn on it. No, one seed of corn is multiplied many times over. In the same way, when we sow ten dollars of seed into good ground, we're not going to get just ten dollars back. God will multiply our seed sown, and He will increase the fruits of our righteousness.

As believers, each one of us has right standing with God through the shed blood of Jesus. That right standing with God should produce fruit in our lives. The fruit of righteousness is the same as the fruit of the Spirit, which includes love, joy, peace, gentleness, and goodness. God will increase the fruit of our righteousness and increase and multiply the seed we've sown when we obey His teachings. He'll meet all of our needs and even give us extra seed to plant for other harvests.

However, we must sow before we can reap a harvest. We must plant the seed before it can grow and produce fruit. I'm continually amazed at the number of people who don't have a good understanding of the principles of sowing and reaping. In order to harvest the crop you desire, the sower must know what the seed is and how to plant it.

The Bible uses the term *sower* to describe someone who is willing to scatter seed liberally, not drop just one little seed here and there.

A liberal sower doesn't place just one seed into the ground and come back a little later to see if it's sprouted. Then after

132

seeing the first seed sprout, take another seed and put it back into the ground. A liberal sower wants to scatter seed everywhere there's good ground. He has a liberal approach to life; he is a giver. He's going to meet someone's needs liberally, providing seed that will increase and multiply for the kingdom of God and for himself. This is the action of a liberal sower.

Oh, you may not like to hear that, and you might be thinking to yourself, *Boy, I sure have a hard time with this. I've worked hard for my money, and I've spent years saving and investing it. I don't want to just give it away.*

DEVELOPING A GIVING HEART

Becoming a good manager of our seed depends on the condition of our heart. We can't tithe or sow seeds liberally if our attitude isn't right. When God says He'll open heaven's windows and pour out a blessing so big there's not room enough to store it (Malachi 3:10), He's saying that if we'll trust Him and tithe with a glad heart, He will overflow blessings upon us.

When God blesses us like that, it somehow works a change in our heart, causing us to love giving even more. Start tithing, and God will enlarge your heart. See if it doesn't change the way you approach money; soon you'll be a liberal sower.

God will trust the liberal sower with more seed. But if we don't have a scattering attitude, He's not going to give us seed just to keep and use on ourselves however we please.

Our goal is that of managing seed. First, remember that the seed isn't money; it's the Word of God. Second, remember that the best way for us to spread seed if we're not a preacher is to use our money to support others who preach the Word. And the third thing to remember is that we must be willing to scatter the seed, because God will meet our needs by multiplying the seed we've sown.

If we use our money to further the preaching of the Gospel, we're going to reap benefits.

WHERE TO SOW

Most of us probably don't stand before masses of people, and we probably don't have the opportunity to spread the Word as someone who is called to a public speaking ministry does. So, giving to those whom God has called to reach the larger numbers of people will multiply our seed. We can communicate God's principles on a one-on-one basis by telling others about Jesus, and when we do this, we're entitled to expect a harvest. However, since the greatest impact on our harvest in life is produced by what we do with our money, we should use it where it will provide the greatest impact in meeting people's needs.

What exactly do people need the most? How do we truly meet human need? These questions must be answered correctly if we are going to simplify our lives by properly managing our seed. When we approach these questions from a spiritual perspective, it's apparent that most people don't need a plate of cookies, a blanket, or even grocery money. The Bible says again and again that it's God Himself who makes the difference in a person's life. God and His Word are the life changers.

Remember, God expects us to be good managers over our seed. So be careful of what ministries you support, and don't be deceived. Familiarize yourself with their doctrine before you give into their ministry. This will also indicate to you the type of soil you're sowing into. There are many different kinds of soil in which to sow your seed. Some soil is hard and won't receive the seed at all. Other soil is so stony it prevents the seed from taking root. Each kind of soil describes the condition of the minister's heart and also the ministry you're sowing your seeds into.

The best soil to plant seed into is the place where you're being fed God's Word. If it's not good soil, find another place that teaches the Word of God. If it is good soil, stay there and be faithful. God places each of us in the body of Christ to grow and continue in good works. He knows what the financial needs of a particular ministry are, and He may want to bless it through your giving.

We are called to plant tithe in the church God leads us to join, but sometimes He will direct us to sow seed elsewhere. That's all right, but the bulk of our sowing should be given to the place where we're taught on a regular basis.

In Corinth, Paul and his team of ministers planted and watered the seed, but God gave the increase. (1 Corinthians 3:6,7) Afterward, Paul said, "If we have sown unto you spiritual

things, is it a great thing if we shall reap your carnal things?"
(1 Corinthians 9:11).

An ongoing exchange occurs when we sow seed into a ministry. The financial support coming from the Corinthians enabled Paul's ministry team to keep preaching and, in turn, allowed the Corinthians to continue receiving spiritual deposits from God. This cycle benefited both parties.

This is God's mode of provision for His people. When we begin producing fruit in our own lives, we are blessed so we can bless others. We are to plug into the place which God has directed us and act as His hands, feet, and mouthpiece. Remember, He doesn't make us healthy and prosperous so we can become couch potatoes. He wants us healthy and prosperous so we can be more effective doing the work of the ministry.

The Bible says, "Who goeth a warfare any time at his own charges? who planteth a vineyard, and eateth not of the fruit thereof? or who feedeth a flock, and eateth not of the milk of the flock?" (1 Corinthians 9:7). The Greek word to describe the feeding of the flock is *poimaino*. It's the same word translated as "pastor" in other parts of the Bible, but the word literally means "to feed, spiritually."

The church God leads us to serve in—the place where we receive spiritual food that will change our life—is to partake of the fruit of our labor. There is to be an exchange of the natural for the supernatural. Scripture is clear on this point. Not only are we supposed to plant our seed where God has assigned us, but we are also supposed to receive spiritual seed that will continue to make our life grow.

Also, I think it's important to give to the "fathers of faith"; namely, those ministers who have forged and pioneered the tenets of the Church. But seeding is primarily meant to be a divine exchange between you and your church. When you're plugged in and consistently fed the Word of God, then you've found the best soil in which to plant your seed. Plant it where the Word is being preached. Scatter it liberally, exercise your faith, and expect a bountiful harvest!

CONNECTING WITH INCREASE

The importance of managing your seed begins with an attitude that understands it's only as we give people the Word of God that we most effectively meet their needs. The needs of people who are unsaved are first and foremost met by introducing them to Jesus. The diverse needs of those who are saved are best met when we teach them the Word of God, because then they can grow and mature in the promises of God. When received and acted upon, the promises of God will begin to meet needs in every area of a believer's life.

We must work hard at that which is good. We must begin to properly manage our expenses and begin honoring God through the vehicle of the tithe. But the final step in properly managing our resources for the purpose of simplifying our lives is to properly manage our seed by using it to meet human need through the preaching of the Word of God. We then connect with God's plan for increase, and the result is supernaturally simplifying our lives in the financial arena!

MANAGING YOUR RELATIONSHIPS

Relationships affect our lives like no other resource. Our friends have the potential to influence us for greatness and godliness, and we can influence other people in the same way.

How do your actions affect other people? It's very important to establish a clear-cut goal or objective when it comes to relationships. You might ask yourself, "What am I in this relationship for? What purpose is it serving?" In my opinion, the single most important reason to form any relationship is to influence someone for God.

Many people approach life with the attitude of tending to their own business unless God happens to plop somebody in their path that He wants them to minister to. Then, if they have the courage, they might share their faith.

Unfortunately, we don't often think in terms of influencing others for God as the basis for getting involved in relationships. In this paraphrase of the great commission, Jesus said, "Go ye into all of the world and preach the Gospel." (Matthew 28:19) That means those who aren't saved need to hear about Jesus.

We should always think about being a godly influence in the lives of those we meet. But don't confuse godly influence with manipulation. We're not called to manipulate others into the kingdom of God. We are supposed to influence the world for God, not manipulate it for Him. Influencing people for God involves helping them prepare their heart attitude to receive Jesus. Anyone who genuinely receives the Lord can say that he or she has been positively influenced, not manipulated. Influence prepares the way for evangelism. Without influencing the world we live in, God's kingdom won't increase and grow.

Relationships are to be based on the love of God that's been shed abroad in our heart by the Holy Spirit. But if our interest in meeting and cultivating a relationship with someone is motivated by a desire for personal gain, then we have just done a severe disservice to that person by manipulating them rather than influencing them for good. Manipulation will always complicate your life, never simplify it.

It all comes down to motive. If we are motivated by love and not by self-interest, then any relationship we get involved in is not likely to become manipulative or deceptive. If our heart's desire is simply to make people aware of the good news that has changed our lives so they can benefit by it, then we shouldn't have to be too concerned about our influence by becoming manipulative or somehow deceptive.

If we don't exercise a godly influence over others, our quality of life will suffer dramatically.

Think about this for a moment. God uses people to bring provision and blessing to our lives. Whether our need is emotional, physical, spiritual, or financial—He uses people to bless us.

When we need encouragement or exhortation, it isn't likely that God will appear in a white, puffy cloud and say, "Be thou encouraged, My child." God sends people to encourage us. And, if we need financial help, He's not going to drop a bag of coins from heaven on our heads. Instead, He'll put it on somebody's heart to supply the need we have.

However, if we've mismanaged our relationships and allowed, say, unforgiveness to remain, then God is limited in what He can do for us. As a result, our own quality of life will suffer. The person we're at odds with may be the one God wants to use to meet our needs. But if we've spoken badly of them or refused to forgive them, how can God help us?

The management of our relationships will certainly affect and impact our quality of life. So again, don't allow yourself to be motivated by selfish concern.

As I said before, I believe the ultimate goal for cultivating relationships with others is to exert as much godly influence as possible. We want to influence our kids to serve God. We want to influence our husband or wife to move closer to God. We want to influence our friends and family to get saved and stay out of harm's way. And we want to see this nation return to the godly principles that it was founded on. That's what relationship management is all about.

MANAGE WITH LOVE

Successfully managing relationships by using the highest degree of godly influence toward others will help to govern our actions by one simple practice—walking in love. It's a spiritual tool which the Bible says never fails. (1 Corinthians 13:8)

The word *love* is a well-worn but little-understood word. I say little understood because there's so much evidence of relationship mismanagement that it suggests we don't have the message of love nailed down yet. On the whole, many of us are not really that good at operating in the love walk. As a pastor, I see the evidence.

There is no greater gift we can possess than the ability to love people the way God does. It's the surest way to generate a godly level of influence with others.

The best one-word summary I can give that relates to our challenge of managing relationships is love. It is the single most powerful resource available to any of us. God says love never fails and it fulfills all the law. Love releases the power to bring circumstantial change.

Faith is a great tool for changing negative circumstances. The Bible says all things are possible to him who believes. (Mark 9:23) God wants us to get ahold of the revelation of the exceeding greatness of His power to us who believe. (Ephesians 1:19) Undoubtedly, faith generates great power, but it still needs one other thing in order to work. The Bible says faith works by love. (Galatians 5:6)

142

Faith requires love. God isn't going to let you simply experience His great flow of power only to be selfish with it. Love focuses us outward, and that's why God says faith works by love.

Love is the greatest spiritual tool we have available in the area of relationship management. Make no mistake about it; the reason for the greatest absence of power in the body of Christ, in my opinion, isn't due to a lack of faith, it's due to a lack of love. Most people I encounter have heard enough of God's Word to begin believing for their petitions. But some don't have their answer because of insufficient love. People can hear the Word day in and day out, twenty-four hours a day, and become a reservoir of God's power. But they won't be able to change their circumstance until their life is governed by love. Love releases the flow of power. Love is the key to successful relationship management.

The more I learn about love, the more I realize how little I really know.

First of all, the kind of love I'm talking about isn't the human love of friendship or romance we talk about so often. That is usually associated with a feeling or an emotion we sometimes call affection. Sometimes there are sexual overtones with this feeling, and sometimes there are not. The kind of love I'm talking about isn't rooted in feelings or emotions.

Some people are just easier to love than others, so we tend to love people on a selective basis instead of unconditionally.

The moment we encounter somebody who's not as attractive as we'd like, or who doesn't smell as nice as we'd like, or who isn't as polite to us as we'd like, we tend to withdraw the love we should extend to him or her, and that doesn't please God.

Aren't you glad God's love is not selective like human love? Aren't you glad God didn't wait to send Jesus until we got our act together? Aren't you glad God's love isn't conditional?

The love of God is unconditional, whereas our love is so often based on conditions. I don't care what somebody looks like, smells like, talks like, acts like, or treats us like—we must make the decision to relate to him or her on the basis of unconditional love. God's love is unconditional, and we are to learn to be like Him.

God's unconditional love is "agape" love. *Agape* means "to value and esteem; affection or benevolence."[1] It expresses the deep and constant love and interest of a perfect Being toward entirely unworthy objects. It's also called the "God-kind of love," because the Bible uses that word to describe how He so loved the world that He gave Jesus. (John 3:16) In many places in the New Testament, it's translated as "charity."

God's love is the kind of love that gives rather than takes. It's the kind of love that makes relationships work.

The God-kind of love gives time, prayer, help, support, encouragement, acceptance, and whatever else is needed. It's the kind of approach to a relationship that makes you a resource to somebody instead of a consumer.

Nevertheless, that's still just a surface definition. It's hard to really define the love of God because we can't completely understand it. To truly understand the love of God, we must study the behavior His love will generate.

First Corinthians 13, the love chapter, gives us the standard by which to measure our lives. We should read it regularly and ask ourselves, "Did I act in love yesterday or this morning? Did I consider others' needs above my own, or was I selfish?" If we need to, we should repent for not walking in love and make some changes.

When we're walking in love, our behavior will bear it out. If we're managing our relationships on the basis of God's love, others will know it. When we're walking in love toward others, we'll be able to exercise the greatest level of godly influence over them.

> *Charity suffereth long, and is kind; charity envieth not; charity vaunteth not itself, is not puffed up, doth not behave itself unseemly, seeketh not her own, is not easily provoked, thinketh no evil; rejoiceth not in iniquity, but rejoiceth in the truth; beareth all things, believeth all things, hopeth all things, endureth all things. Charity never faileth.*
>
> 1 Corinthians 13:4-8

Let's look at the same passage in the Amplified translation. While you're reading it, ask yourself, "Does this describe my typical approach to other people?" If it doesn't, you are mismanaging your relationships and you won't influence people in the way God would have you influence them.

> *Love endures long and is patient and kind; love never is envious nor boils over with jealousy, is not boastful or vainglorious,*

does not display itself haughtily. It is not conceited (arrogant and inflated with pride); it is not rude (unmannerly) and does not act unbecomingly. Love (God's love in us) does not insist on its own rights or its own way, for it is not self-seeking; it is not touchy or fretful or resentful; it takes no account of the evil done to it [it pays no attention to a suffered wrong]. It does not rejoice at injustice and unrighteousness, but rejoices when right and truth prevail. Love bears up under anything and everything that comes, is every ready to believe the best of every person, its hopes are fadeless under all circumstances, and it endures everything [without weakening]. Love never fails [never fades out or becomes obsolete or comes to an end].

1 Corinthians 13:4-8 Amp.

Does your behavior toward others measure up to this? When it says "love is patient," do you give people time to grow? Do you become aggravated with the proverbial one-year-old Christian who's not walking yet as you think he or she should be?

Do you get impatient when your kids don't clean up their rooms when you ask? We have to give people a chance to grow both naturally and spiritually. Quite often, it's easier to let them grow up naturally but not spiritually. It's necessary to be patient with others while they're growing up. Love is patient and kind.

To be kind means to be good to others. It could be an act of kindness or a word of encouragement. It could be a simple act like opening the car door for your wife for the first time in twenty years. Or it could be the act of just being thoughtful toward others. Kindness is an extension of the love of God.

Love is never envious and doesn't boil over with jealousy. (1 Corinthians 13:4 Amp.) Maybe you don't have a problem with envy and jealousy, but there are always those who seem to be competitive—just a little.

We probably wouldn't care too much if a perfect stranger beat us in a game of ping-pong or tennis, but if it were our brother or our father—that's a little bit different! We might tend to excuse ourself for this behavior, by saying, "I'm really not jealous about things in general." But we forget about the few people who make us feel a little competitive until they beat us here or there at something, and then the jealousy stirs up.

According to God's definition of love, that's not allowed, because it's an occasion to mismanage a potentially very important relationship. Be certain jealousy is not present in your life, and be honest in your self-examination.

"Love...is not boastful or vainglorious [and] does not display itself haughtily" (1 Corinthians 13:4 Amp.). I think that pertains to men more than anyone else. Guys tend to boast a little bit more than women, and, in a kidding way, they tend to talk about how great they are. But it's an attitude that both men and women need to adjust, because it opens the door to something that can rob us of fruitful and productive relationships.

"[Love] is not conceited (arrogant and inflated with pride); it is not rude (unmannerly) and does not act unbecomingly" (1 Corinthians 13:5 Amp.). What happens when the telemarketer calls right in the middle of dinner? Has that ever happened to any of you? Sure it has. Most of us have had a bad experience with a telemarketer at one time or another.

I've had one. I remember one time a telemarketer called and he wouldn't even let me finish my sentence. I tried to say, "I'm sorry. I'm not..." but he wouldn't stop. A few minutes later I said, "Really, I don't think... No, I'm not... No, I don't want...." Finally, I just blew him off, acted rudely, and hung up the phone. Afterward, I wondered if he knew I was a pastor. Unfortunately, I didn't influence him toward godliness.

The Lord really used that occasion to speak to me. He showed me the need to be more mindful to exercise godly influence over others, turning what could be occasions for rudeness into opportunities for godliness. Now I approach tele-marketers differently. When I get a telephone call from them now, I simply interrupt and say something such as this: "Now, wait a minute. You've made an unsolicited call to my home. Now, I will open myself up to what you want to say, if you will first listen to what I want to say."

Do you know that I've never heard any of them say no to this? Remember, they're calling me. I've got a captive audi-ence, and now I can say, "I'll listen to you, but you're going to listen to me first. Are you saved? Are you going to heaven or hell?"

You know what's funny about that? I don't get very many telemarketing calls anymore. Satan doesn't harass me that way, because he knows they're going to get a good dose of Jesus!

The point is this: If we don't look at these interruptions as chances to exercise godly influence, we'll miss opportunities to influence people toward godliness. When I rudely cut myself off from that telemarketer, I also cut off my opportunity to exercise a godly influence over him. I wasn't acting in love.

"[Love] is not self-seeking; it is not touchy or fretful or resentful; it takes no account of the evil done to it" (1 Corinthians 13:5 Amp.). I wish I had a nickel for every time somebody said to me, "Pastor, you just don't know what he did to me." Well, if we are as loving as we should be, we wouldn't take notice. God says love takes no account of it.

Think about the last time you were offended. Most of the time people don't mean to offend, but even if they did, we are supposed to take no account of the evil done to us. In so doing, we will be a much more positive influence on others than if we had fought with them. Ultimately, we will feel a lot better too.

"[Love] does not rejoice at injustice and unrighteousness" (1 Corinthians 13:6 Amp.). This reminds me of more than one occasion when I was tempted to call attention to someone else's suffering after he or she did something wrong. It would have been easy to say, "Look! The fire of God got them. See there! They're just getting what they deserve," especially if that person had been particularly ugly. Usually there's a little bit of pleasure inside us when this happens, but it's wrong to think this way. The result would be a damaged relationship and limited opportunity to be a godly influence.

We mismanage our relationships when we rejoice at someone else's pain, whether the pain is justified or not. We're supposed to rejoice when truth prevails, not when injustice prevails.

"Love bears up under anything and everything that comes, is ever ready to believe the best of every person" (1 Corinthians 13:7 Amp.). What are you believing? Do you believe what the people around you are saying? Begin with your kids. Are you believing they're going to make A's this next quarter and encouraging them in this? Are you saying to them, "I believe you can earn that 'A' because you have the mind of Christ. I rejoice with you over your next report card"? Are you believing the best for everything your kids do?

Love believes the best about everyone. (1 Corinthians 13:7) When people tell you something, do you find yourself automatically believing they're lying or perhaps misrepresenting the facts a little? What do you believe? Well, if you've grown up like most of us, you're protecting your backside. If we're believing the worst to protect ourselves, that's wrong. When we project that kind of thinking into a relationship, it won't prosper. We must change our approach and begin believing the best about others, not the worst. When we start to believe the best, it will begin to show in our conversations, in the way we relate to others and in the way we are able to influence their lives for God.

I like what the Message Bible has to say about God's love.

Love never gives up. Love cares more for others than for self. Love doesn't want what it doesn't have. Love doesn't strut. Doesn't have a swelled head. Doesn't force itself on others. Isn't always me first. Doesn't fly off the handle. Doesn't keep score of the sins of others. Doesn't revel when others grovel, takes pleasure in the flowering of truth. Puts up with anything. Trusts God always. Always looks for the best. Never looks back. Keeps going to the end. Love never fails.

1 Corinthians 13:4-8 Msg.

This passage of Scripture shows us our potential as Christians. We have the capacity to walk in love like this when the Holy Spirit sheds the love of God abroad in our hearts. This isn't something we can automatically say we're going to accomplish by discipline and self-control. Walking in love is a process; it's not something we change overnight. Thirty years of bad behavior doesn't change immediately. And we can't begin managing relationships in a completely different way at the drop of a hat.

Walking in love toward others is the first step toward better relationship management. It's the tool we use to influence others for God. Without it, we won't be effective at relating to people the way God wants us to.

Remember, our ultimate motive for getting involved in any relationship should be to influence others for God. That's the single most important thing we can do when it comes to managing our relationships with people. We must keep this objective in mind when we begin a relationship with anyone. The more we can influence them for God, the better. And the more successful we are at walking in love toward others, the easier our relationships will be to manage.

TWELVE

LOVING GOD AND OTHERS
THE WAY GOD LOVES YOU

We have seen that the primary reason we are to manage relationships correctly is to exercise the greatest amount of godly influence possible in the lives of people around us.

This is a clear biblical mandate for every believer. The Lord didn't just tell us to preach the Gospel to all the world. (Mark 16:15) He also instructed us to be a light unto the world. (Matthew 5:16) We are to reach them *and* teach them.

A light is something that is seen by others; it guides them and shows the way. As lights unto the world, we must strive to manage our relationships well.

If we mismanage them, one of four outcomes will be the result. We will either fail to influence others for good, we won't influence others at all, or we'll influence others in the wrong way.

The fourth possible outcome is worst of all. It is possible that by mismanaging relationships, *we* can be the ones who are influenced—and in the wrong direction! That's why we have to be proactive in this area by deliberately pursuing the goal of influencing others, because it won't happen automatically. This is what relationship skills are all about.

In addition to helping others, there are important personal benefits. God will use the relationships we cultivate to bring His direction, His provision, His encouragement, and His blessing to bear in our lives. God will use other people in our lives to bless us.

Occasionally, we may have a vision or a dream where God may minister to us independently of other people, but most of the time, He uses other people. We are part of the body of Christ in the earth, and as such, we're connected to others. He chooses to give us encouragement, direction, and whatever else we need through other people. And because relationships are made up of people, they sometimes can get kind of tricky. As we all know, people have emotions and opinions of all kinds that may or may not be good for cultivating a godly relationship. That's where God's love comes in. We have to put love into action for it to be effective. We have to turn love into our normal behavior in order to influence others for God.

This is not something we accomplish just by disciplining ourselves. It's not a matter of exercising a sufficient amount of self-will to modify our behavior. There is a simple but profound truth involved in becoming a lover of God and men. It involves loving ourself and others the way God loves us.

I've said it before: Love is the most significant spiritual tool you can possess to cultivate and manage your relationships with others. The Bible clearly says that love never fails. (1 Corinthians 13:8) Therefore, if we have a relationship that's giving us a problem, that doesn't always indicate there's something wrong with the other person. It may be telling us there's something wrong with *our* love walk.

If we can learn the secrets of love that God reveals to us in the Word, then our relationships will prosper too. As we walk in love toward others, God will then have many channels to bring His provision and blessing into our lives. Our lives will become much less complicated, and the overall quality of our lives will be considerably elevated.

Realize this: If our relationships aren't working, there is only one person we have the power to change. Take that big index finger and point it right back at yourself. It's true, friend. The only person on the face of this earth we have the power to change is ourselves.

Since love never fails, if we learn the lessons of love, we will cultivate healthy, lasting relationships that will not fail.

I realize that is a hard truth for some people to swallow, but it is a biblical truth nonetheless.

Now, don't misunderstand. I'm not an advocate of people staying in close proximity to a person who is physically abusive. That's not what I'm saying here. Some people need to be loved from a distance.

What I am saying is that walking in love is the most basic concern in managing and cultivating relationships with others.

One of the reasons God's love works so well is that it's not rooted in human emotion. The God-kind of love is not a feeling. Most of the time, human love is thought of as something that one feels. The secular world, for the most part, applies a sexual connotation to it as well. Consequently, many people in the world have no real concept of what this kind of love is.

The thing that becomes clearest to us when we make the decision to love others is that it's impossible to truly love in our own strength. We cannot discipline our behavior enough to conform to God's standard of love by using willpower alone. We cannot be determined enough to do this all the time without ever slipping up. Being an iron-willed person just isn't enough.

We can't love the way God requires unless there's a change inside of us. I'm not talking about getting saved, because we all have the potential to walk in love when we're saved. The Bible says the love of God is shed abroad in our hearts by the Holy Spirit. (Romans 5:5) We didn't have this capacity before we were saved, but we received it afterward. We could act nice on occasion, but we had no capacity to love as God does until we were saved.

However, the fact that we're saved doesn't mean the love that's in our heart automatically becomes the guiding standard for relationship management. Our behavioral tendencies don't automatically change just because we get saved. Something else has to occur in our heart for this kind of love to affect the way we treat others and manage relationships with people around us. We must become a lover along the lines of God's definition of the word.

Jesus said, "As the Father hath loved me, so have I loved you: continue ye in my love" (John 15:9). Jesus was able to love us because He first saw the pattern demonstrated through the Father's love for Him.

We can't love another person beyond our own level of understanding of the love God has for us.

I'm not talking about defining love as we do in human terms. Most of us can say, "Well, yes, I know God loves this person and that person, and, of course, me too." But thinking of God's love in these terms doesn't begin to describe His love for us. God's love is unconditional.

So often we express our love conditionally toward others, even when we don't mean to. Our love is often reserved, or set aside, for those people who please us. We love people when they meet our expectation, as if somehow they must earn it.

Aren't you glad that's not true of the Lord? The Bible says that "God commendeth his love toward us, in that, while we were yet sinners, Christ died for us" (Romans 5:8). That means that God didn't wait until we were attractive to love us. He didn't wait until we were all born again and pretty to love us. Aren't you glad He didn't wait until you got your act together to send Jesus? This is how God loves us and how we are to love others. This is where it begins, but we must first have a revelation of the depth of God's love for us before we can act it out.

Did you know that most people do not know this kind of love? I would estimate that over 90 percent of the people sitting in church on any given Sunday morning do not truly know how much God loves them. Oh, they can mentally or intellectually affirm that they do, agreeing that this is a basic truth of Christianity, but they don't have a revelation of it.

"God so loved the world, that he gave..." (John 3:16). Well, you're included in that statement. Yes, you may know God loves you, but do you really have a revelation of the depth of God's love for you? Because if you don't, you cannot love anybody else the way God wants you to.

And we have known and believed the love that God hath to us. God is love; and he that dwelleth in love dwelleth in God, and God in him. Herein is our love made perfect, that we may have boldness in the day of judgment: because as he is, so are we in this world. There is no fear in love; but perfect love casteth out fear.

1 John 4:16-18

Here is another biblical validation of the truth that our love matures only to the degree that we know and accept the love God has for us. Our love is "made perfect" because we have "known" and "believed" God loves us. Our ability to love others will mature as we come to know and believe that God loves us unconditionally.

Notice how the Amplified translation phrases it: "And we know, (understand, recognize, are conscious of, by observation and by experience) and believe (adhere to and put faith in and rely on) the love God cherishes for us" (1 John 4:16 Amp.).

To have a revelation of God's love we must "know," "understand," "recognize," "be conscious of," "experience," "believe," "adhere to," "put faith in," and "rely on" God's love—the love He "cherishes for us."

Sadly, most people don't have a revelation of this kind of love to any significant degree, and yet the Bible says in the next verse, "Herein is our love made perfect" (1 John 4:17).

We need to ask God to show us the specific barriers that keep us from receiving this kind of revelation. I know I'm not there in my own life. I still struggle conceptually with the idea of this kind of love. Intellectually, I can believe it's true. I read it in the Bible, and I believe it. But I'm talking about having a heart-revelation of this kind of love.

This is precisely at the heart of what Paul prayed for the Ephesian believers:

> ...that ye, being rooted and grounded in love, may be able to comprehend with all saints what is the breadth, and length, and depth and height; and to know the love of Christ, which passeth knowledge.
>
> Ephesians 3:17-19

I hope there are people in your life whose love for you is such a settled issue that it's not something you ever question. You may have friends whom you can go to and ask anything, knowing they would help you in any way.

It might be your mother or father, your husband or wife. Hopefully, there's somebody whose love for you has been so consistently demonstrated that you never question it. You can go to this person even in the darkest moments of your life and they will be there for you.

God wants to be there that way for you. Most people don't have that kind of intimacy with Him. We don't have that revelation of God's love, in part, because we know ourselves better than anybody else does. We know all of our shortcomings and hang-ups—and we usually rehearse them to ourselves often.

I know how despicable I've been on occasion. I know the things I've done in my past that I'm ashamed of—some things that no one else knows about except the Lord. I know how very flawed I still am. And sometimes it's this kind of intimacy with the Lord that makes it so hard to understand how such a holy, omniscient Being, who knows all this about me, can still love me—and without reservation.

We have to *believe* that God loves us this much. Our quality of life depends on it. Our ability to have a happy marriage, to enjoy quality friendships, to influence other people for God, and to cultivate relationships based on love depends upon our understanding and believing that God loves us like that.

In every relationship problem I have ever encountered as a minister, I can trace the problem back, in one form or another, to insecurity in one or both of the two parties involved. At its root is insecurity in the knowledge of God's love for them. Insecurity to such a degree that makes it impossible for people to relate to each other stems from an insufficient understanding of the depth of God's love for them.

The insecurity issue would be settled once and for all with a sufficient understanding of God's love, because the Bible says, "There is no fear in love; but perfect love casteth out fear" (1 John 4:18).

Let me show you another liberating aspect of this truth. If you are tormented by fear in any form—anxiety, oppression, worry—you need a revelation of God's love for you. Worry is fear, you know. We can't worry about something apart from fear, because worry is a form of fear. Where we identify the presence of fear in our life, we're not perfected in love. Perfect love casts out fear. Love and fear cannot coexist. Therefore, if we're not perfected in love, it means we haven't experienced a revelation of God's love for ourselves. Think about all of this for a moment.

If you're perfected or mature in love, you won't fear. You will be one bold individual. You won't care what anybody thinks about you. With a good grasp on perfected love, you can tell people whatever they need to hear without regard for the consequences. I'm not talking about being rude or unmannerly, but being bold. First Corinthians 13 tells us that love isn't rude. But perfected love is not fearful of rejection either. That's why it gives us the power to tell people the truth. We can become bold witnesses when we're perfected in love.

When we're perfected in love, the doctor's report doesn't cause us to go into a panic or a deep depression. When we're perfected in love, financial challenges don't cause fear to rise up in our heart.

Instead, we rejoice that we're delivered from this world's economy. When we're perfected in love, fear has no hold on our life, and we can become a world-changer. When we're perfected in love, we'll be a person who influences other people for God.

We're not going to influence anybody in a positive way for God if our life is controlled by fear. But, thank God, perfect love casts out fear! When you get ahold of the revelation that God's love for you is unconditional, you can be as bold as a lion.

BE THE DISCIPLE
WHO LOVED JESUS

Do you remember the apostle John? He was the only disciple who really had this kind of revelation of God's unconditional love for him. He constantly described himself as the disciple whom Jesus loved. Do you want to see how that revelation produced a difference between John and the other disciples? John followed Jesus to the cross when He was being crucified, but Peter separated himself from the Lord because of fear. John followed Jesus, and when Jesus was about to die, completing His work on the earth, to whom did He entrust the care of his mother? John. Who is the only apostle who didn't die a martyr's death? John.

All the other apostles died as martyrs, but not John. They tried to boil him in oil, but they couldn't kill him. Finally, they banished him to the Isle of Patmos hoping it would drive him insane and he would die, but that didn't work either. Instead, he received the revelation of the end times and wrote the book of Revelation.

Being secure in the love of God casts out all fear and opens us to a level of blessing that is otherwise unattainable. Think about it. When we know how much God, the Creator of the universe, loves us, we're not going to be bothered by any of the nitpicky little things that most of the world trembles at.

We can laugh in the face of disaster because we know God loves us. We can laugh at Satan because we know God's not going to let him overpower us. What a revelation!

Many people will never have a clue about God's love for them unless it comes through people like you and me who have had a revelation of God's love.

Initially, most people sense the love of God when it comes through the touch of a yielded believer. Our ability to influence others the right way and to manage and cultivate good relationships with others depends on understanding God's love for us.

As a pastor, one of the things that really excites me is to see this kind of understanding come to somebody who, perhaps, was on his deathbed when God touched him and raised him up. The most overwhelming result of this kind of touch from God is revelation not only of God's power, but of His love.

I've seen people delivered from drugs and alcohol upon discovering this wondrous truth. Those people could then begin to love others, because they had experienced it first-hand. They were free to go out and love others who are in the same situation they once were in.

Now, don't get me wrong. You don't have to go through a life-threatening crisis to understand how much God loves you. This is part of the good news. We don't have to get to the bottom of whatever barrel Satan may be trying to stuff us into in order to suddenly have a revelation of the love of God.

There are a couple of things we can do to position ourselves in a way that will enable God to bring that revelation to bear in our lives.

God is not interested in keeping it a secret, and He doesn't want us to be in the dark about it. He wants us to know how much He loves us, and He wants to show it to us in terms so simple that a small child can grasp it.

Although it's simplistic, it's profoundly true. Unfortunately, that's one of the primary reasons many people never receive this kind of revelation from God. They're too prideful to receive the simple truth that "God is love" (1 John 4:8).

FELLOWSHIPING WITH GOD

God can't reveal anything to us if we never give Him the time to do it, and most people don't. For most, if they have a devotional life at all, it's only to toss Him a little laundry list of requests on the way out the door.

I'm not necessarily talking about baby Christians. Some mature believers take time to read the Word only five minutes before they go to bed for the night, then they wonder why the love of God never seems to touch their heart like it does other people.

Fellowship is the prerequisite to receiving this revelation from God. He can't reveal anything to us if we don't give Him the opportunity.

Fellowship, as you may know, consists of two elements. It requires both the Word of God and communion with Him through prayer. One without the other doesn't get the job done. God's Word reveals God to us. It's impossible to know very much about God without reading His Word. That's where it begins. And if a revelation of the love of God is something you're pursuing, then you need to read the Word, especially where it refers to your place of importance with Him. You will be transformed by renewing your mind in this area. (Romans 12:2)

If you want to know how special you are to God, you might start by doing word studies and digging out the Scriptures that will confirm in your heart that you are important to Him. Find out how much He loves you, and then begin confessing that Word. Listen to that Word and get it down into your heart, because faith comes by hearing.

Deal a death blow to the inferiority and insecurity that hampers so many people in their walk with God. Get in the Word; that's where it all begins.

Once you've found Scriptures to affirm your importance to God, begin communing with Him in prayer.

My own experience might be helpful to you in this regard. Early on in my walk with the Lord, after I realized I needed to spend some devotional time with Him, I started reading the Word and then praying afterward. At that time, my prayers consisted mostly of making confessions that were consistent with the fruit I wanted to see in my life.

Then, of course, I had a laundry list of "God-do's." You know what God-do's are, don't you? They are "God, please do this. God, I need You to do that." God-do's and my laundry list are what I started out with.

That was the essence of my prayer life back then, but I had to get beyond that to pursue the presence and the person of God. He wants us to seek after Him, and not just when we have needs He can meet. It's not wrong to begin a prayer life by asking for God's help in various areas of our lives, but we also need to grow and move into other levels of communion with Him.

At first, I found it very hard to devote time to prayer and communion with God. It seemed that there were so many other things I wanted to do besides get still before the Lord. (Remember those distractions we talked about at the beginning of this book?)

I didn't have as much of a desire to get quiet before the Lord as I did to do some other things. I wanted to do other good things, of course, not bad things, but I didn't have the intense desire to stay focused on communion with God. I can remember telling my wife, Lynne, that she was called to pray and I wasn't. I used that as my excuse.

I would say something like, "Boy, I wish I had your desire to just be with God. It would make things a whole lot easier for me if I just had that desire." My time with God often seemed dry and nonproductive. I wanted more desire, but I just didn't have it.

I eventually learned that we will create an appetite for those things we give attention to. This is a scriptural truth. That's why the Lord says, *Don't love or give yourself to the things of the world.* (1 John 2:15) The love of God doesn't reside in the person who does.

When the love for worldly things becomes our focus, our appetite for those things will increase. We'll be filled with a desire for the things we have an appetite for. That's a spiritual law. Therefore, we have to cultivate an appetite and a hunger for God by giving our attention to the things of God.

There are dozens of examples in my life of times when I created an appetite for something. For example, I created a desire for a particular sporting activity. I had friends or acquaintances who were involved in it; they hounded me to join, and sometimes I did. Then, whenever I didn't play well, I became annoyed and embarrassed. As a result, I started paying more attention to the sport. After all, I didn't want to lose. I discovered that the more I focused on it, the more of an appetite I developed, and the next thing I knew, I had a strong desire for it. I began liking it more and more.

Attention breeds appetite. Attention to right things breeds right appetites, whereas attention to wrong things breeds wrong appetites. If you have an appetite for the wrong thing, quit giving it attention. The Lord says to not look, or set our hearts, on the physical things we can see because they are temporary and subject to change. (2 Corinthians 4:18)

Don't give attention to ungodly things; don't focus on them. Instead, look at, consider, and focus on the spiritual realm.

Consider the Word of God, because that's where eternity lies. Create an appetite for the things of God, and your desire for them will follow.

Discipline your prayer life; protect that time and make yourself give attention to it. Don't let your mind wander, but instead, focus on and be attentive to the person of the Lord.

Lynne used to say she would envision herself in the arms of the Lord. That brought a lot of comfort to her. It never worked for me, but it worked well for her. What works for me is seeing myself walking and talking with Jesus.

When I have something that challenges me, I will initiate a conversation in my devotional time with the Lord about that challenge. I involve Him in the problem.

When I'm facing what seems like a tough situation, I like to envision my eternal destiny ruling and reigning with Christ. That makes the problem look smaller. Then I envision myself working with God on the problem, and that puts the whole thing into perspective.

I don't know what fits your image and your views of communion with God, but whatever it is, make Him the focus of your attention. Get Him involved on your behalf. Talk to Him for extended periods of time, and the next thing you know, you'll have a hunger for more of Him. Pretty soon, you won't be able to wait to get back to your prayer closet.

The Word says that those who are hungry will be filled. (Matthew 5:6)

You will be filled not only with the presence of God, but with a revelation of His love for you.

Start out by simply fellowshiping with Him through His Word and prayer. If you don't have a desire to do that right now, that can change. Ask God to give you the desire to fellowship more with Him.

The second thing you need to do is to be willing to lay down your life for somebody else. Look at the following Scripture: "Hereby perceive we the love of God, because he laid down his life for us: and we ought to lay down our lives for the brethren" (1 John 3:16).

Here's the way most of us read that verse: *Well, people are going to perceive the love of God by how we serve others and how we lay down our lives for the brethren. That's how people are going to see the love of God.*

But it doesn't say that. The Bible says, "Perceive we the love of God." Here's the point I want to make: When we understand that the Bible requires us to conform to the image and example of Jesus, it means we are to be prepared to lay down our lives for others just as He did.

I believe that to lay down our lives for somebody is the most important thing we can do after being born again. In doing so, we're conforming to the image of Jesus. We're called to be servants, meeting the needs of others. So, when we have this mind-set, it lays an axe to the root of self-interest.

To serve others is to lay down your life for them. But we can't serve until we are modeling our life after what we see

Jesus doing in the Bible. We must get to the place where love compels us to use our resource of life to meet human need, whether it is giving money to support the preaching of the Gospel, serving in the church where God has called us, or sharing our faith with others.

When we make that decision, something happens. When we decide to love others unconditionally by serving their needs, we deal a spiritual deathblow to the root of self-interest. Now God can reveal the depth of His love for us, bringing our ability to love others into perfection or maturity.

Some may feel this is an extreme message. You may be thinking, *You mean, everything I do in life has to be oriented around helping someone else?* Well, friend, if you want your life to be blessed, yes! If you want to go back to the same old ho-hum life you've been living, then don't change.

I'm not saying that we have to spend all our waking hours groveling around in a kind of bondage often equated with slavery. Model your behavior after Jesus and ask for grace to follow through. Search the Scriptures; allow the Holy Spirit to teach and empower you to govern your actions.

It's a privilege to be used by God to serve someone else's need. God honors and blesses us for our service. Decide to be a servant and cultivate a godly love for others. Search the Scriptures and fellowship with God, giving Him an opportunity to reveal the depth of His love for you. Don't allow yourself to be tempted by self-interest.

I believe that the understanding of God's love for us is the most needed revelation in the body of Christ today. When we fellowship with the Lord, we might just find ourselves waking up in the morning exploding with excitement over the knowledge of how important we are to Him. Fear will be gone, and the quality of our relationships will improve. We'll be able to influence others for God as never before. Life will become much less complicated, and we'll begin living the simple life, the good life—the God-kind of life.

THIRTEEN

MANAGING YOUR EMOTIONS

There is no such thing as a neutral relationship.

The very reason God has entrusted us with the circle of acquaintances we have right now is so that we can exercise the greatest degree of godly influence possible over them.

Of course, most people don't approach relationships with this awareness, but the bottom line is the same. That's why God brings us into contact with other people. It's why the Bible says to let your light shine in the darkness of this world. (Matthew 5:16) We are the salt of the earth (Matthew 5:13), and it is our responsibility to be a godly influence in our community.

Every decision a person makes is a reflection of the most powerful influences operating in their life. That's a powerful statement, but it's true. Let me give you an example of what I'm talking about.

When somebody goes out to buy alcohol, drugs, or some other harmful substance, it isn't a casual purchase. That action is the end product of the dominant influence in that person's life. Whether it be good or bad, every person's decisions to do the things he or she does is the result of the accumulated influences in his or her life.

In a very real sense, the good things that we decide to do simply reflect the godly influences we've absorbed into our lives. The bad or destructive things that we do are simply reflective of the presence of ungodly influences in our lives.

That's why we need to take a proactive stance in influencing the people with whom we have relationships. It's the reason God entrusts us with those relationships in the first place. We are to be the best possible managers or stewards over those relationships. But before we can become good stewards, we need to have the right goal for entering into relationships.

As we've seen, the proper goal is to influence others for God. We must practice walking in love toward those we're called to influence for godliness.

Remember, love never fails. (1 Corinthians 13:8) So, if you have a relationship that's failing because of mismanagement that results in a schism or controversy, it is vital to identify what, if anything, you can do to change.

God's love should motivate us to serve others, keeping *their* best interests in mind. If we begin managing our relationships on the basis of God's love, it will open a channel He can use to benefit us and bring blessing and provision into our lives.

Although this is never to be our motive for entering into relationships with others, it's definitely a benefit.

As I've said before, serving others in love has the tendency to significantly elevate the quality of our lives. Whether our need is encouragement, financial help, exhortation, or direction, the Lord is going to use people to bring those things to us.

The extent to which we've managed our relationships properly on the foundation of God's love determines our ability to receive blessings that God gives us to meet our needs. If we're not getting the needs in our lives met, then perhaps we need to start blessing others out of a heart of love.

But before we can genuinely love other people, we must first experience a personal revelation of God's love for us. We cannot love somebody else with a love we've never experienced ourselves. Until we have a revelation and an understanding of the depth of God's love for us, which is the great life-changing experience we can have, we'll never be able to consistently love other people.

That's why 1 John 4:19 NAS says, "We love, because He first loved us."

Most people don't have a clue as to how precious and special they are in the eyes of God.

Knowing how much God loves us forms the basis for loving others consistently and genuinely. When we model our pattern for loving on 1 Corinthians 13, we will fulfill the law of love as Jesus commanded in the New Testament. (John 13:34,35)

LOVING OTHERS EMOTIONALLY

Love is so very important to relationships, it can't be over-stated. We've already looked at how agape love works. Agape love gives like God gives; it's unconditional. But it's important for us to understand another kind of love described in the Bible. The word *love* in the Greek New Testament is used about 160 times. Out of that number, the Greek word *agape* is used about 145 times. And in the rest, the Greek word *phileo,* which refers to the fond emotion or feeling of love, is used. It's a brotherly love, a friendship love.

Every one of us has emotions. We may sometimes wish we didn't have them, but our emotions serve a purpose. God gave us emotions, and they are good. We may view an emotional person as unrestrained, undisciplined, or non-intellectual, and sometimes we may view emotions as a negative thing, but they don't have to be.

God created us with the capacity to feel things emotionally. Our emotions are a part of our soulish realm, which, according to the Bible, is made up of our mind, our will, and our emotions. (1 Thessalonians 5:23) Our emotions contribute to the decisions we make; however, that doesn't mean our decisions have to be made haphazardly. The decision-making process should be deliberate, and it should incorporate all aspects of our soulish realm—intellect, will, and emotions.

Some people tend to make decisions based either solely on their intellect or solely on the way they feel, but neither is right. Ideally, decision making should involve a consolidated process utilizing both aspects.

Intellectually, we have the capacity to esteem, evaluate, and measure all the information at our disposal. Some of that information is obviously going to come through our points of sensory perception. Some of it comes from spiritual information, including the inward witness of the Holy Spirit or the Word of God.

Each of these factors contributes to our ability to examine all the information at hand. Then, on the basis of that process, we can come to a conclusion as to which options would be best and make a decision.

Our emotions are intended to give strength, impetus, and staying power to the decisions we make. God says that if we're double-minded or if we waver, we'll receive nothing from Him. (James 1:6) Our emotions give us the staying power to follow through on a decision we've first made intellectually.

For example, you might be able to come to the intellectual conclusion very easily that it's in your best interest to quit smoking. But it's one thing to decide something intellectually and quite another thing to follow through with it. If your intellect is the only component involved in making that decision, you might quit for a day or two but then go right back to smoking.

You have to get emotionally involved in the decision to quit smoking. You have to become angry. You have to be righteously indignant that Satan has been able to promote some kind of cheap dependence on a stinking tobacco leaf in your life. You need to get mad about that! You have to become so indignant about it that you will apply that indignation to resolve never to do it again. Your emotions will help you do that.

If we don't get emotionally involved in the decision-making process, then we won't be able to drive Satan out of our lives. We'll have a hard time making decisions and sticking with them. This is true for any decision we make.

If you make the decision to love somebody and prefer him or her over everyone else, you're going to need emotions to do it. To have the staying power to be true to one person means you have the emotional capacity to feel affection for him or her. That gives you the ability to keep on giving. Agape love gives, but phileo love sustains that decision to keep on giving.

Let's face it. It's easier to give affection to some people more than to others. Men, think back to the time when you were dating your wife. That affection started to bloom on the inside of you. You couldn't give her enough attention, courtesy, or gifts. You couldn't do enough for her because it's easy to give to somebody you feel affection for.

The key is to keep that affection alive even after marriage. To do so, it's necessary to give affection regardless of how long we have known people or how attractive they look. The ability to sustain phileo love is the key to sustaining your decision to give to other people. It is the very heartbeat of your ability to walk in agape love toward others.

Most people approach affection as something that either happens or it doesn't—thus, the term *falling in love*. They don't realize that love is a learned response and that affection is cultivated.

If you wait for feelings of affection to enter into a relationship, you may end up waiting for a long time. There may be only two or three people among all the relationships God gives you in which you feel affection. The vast majority of your relationships probably don't just spontaneously generate a feeling of affection. You may have to take steps to become an affectionate person; otherwise, you may never be able to consistently give to others.

Let's look at how Jesus characterized phileo love toward His disciples during His earthly ministry.

> *At that day ye shall ask in my name: and I say not unto you, that I will pray the Father for you: For the Father himself loveth you, because ye have loved me, and have believed that I came out from God.*

John 16:26,27

The key to understanding God's desire to give us whatever we ask of Him is found in the use of the word *phileo*. Jesus described God's generosity toward us by using the idea of phileo love, not agape love. By doing this, Jesus is saying that the Father loves us affectionately and tenderly.

Part of getting our prayers answered has to do with believing that Jesus is the Son of God. But beyond believing this, Jesus goes on to describe the bond of love in terms of our emotional response to Him.

In my own life there came a time when I understood I needed a Savior. I decided to believe that Jesus is the Son of God and that He paid the price for my redemption. That's when I did what the Bible told me to do to become a member of the family of God. I believed in my heart that He is Lord, and I made a confession with my mouth, according to Romans 10:9-10.

Even though I did this, Jesus still seemed too remote and impersonal for me to experience any genuine sense of affection for Him. But as time passed, I grew to love the Lord, and I cultivated stronger feelings of affection for Him the more I came to know Him.

You see, because we're made in the image of God, we're a direct reflection of the Father. We bear His image and likeness, and, consequently, His capacity to give and receive affection. The closer we come to the Lord, the more we see our prayers answered.

John 16:23 says, "God will grant you whatever you ask of Him in Jesus' name."

What Jesus meant can be understood when we see it in its context. Many people have asked for things in His name without realizing they were asking for something that was not His will to give. When He doesn't give them their request, they wonder why their prayer wasn't answered.

If we ask for something while we've got a door open to sin in our lives, God won't give us our request. Even though God wants to bless us, He is unable to until we ask according to His will.

Our relationship with God can't be cold, distant, or impersonal, if we want to benefit the way God intends. It is essential to have heartfelt affection for God. The Word says, "Delight thyself also in the Lord; and he shall give thee the desires of thine heart" (Psalms 37:4).

It's this kind of closeness with God that allows you to ask anything of Him in the name of Jesus and expect that it will be done for you.

We can't afford not to be an affectionate (phileo) person. Our ability to walk in God's blessings depends on how well we cultivate an affectionate relationship with Jesus. As we do this, we will become more like Him, and our ability to give to others without limitation will flow out in proportion to our level of affection for God.

If two children who both need something were standing in front of you—one of them being genuinely and sincerely affectionate, telling you how much she loves you all the time, and the other one being indifferent, showing up every now and then with her hand out—who would you rather give to?

I think we could all agree that we'd be more inclined to give to the affectionate one.

LOVE THE LORD OR BE CURSED

No matter what we do, the Lord still loves us. He may not be pleased with some of our actions, but if we're a child of His, He loves us unconditionally. And it's extremely important that we love the Lord. The Bible says, "If anyone does not love the Lord [does not have a friendly affection for Him and is not kindly disposed toward Him], he shall be accursed!" (1 Corinthians 16:22 Amp.). Now, that's heavy!

You might think, *Does that mean if I don't love the Lord, He's going to zap me with a curse like a lightning bolt from heaven?* No!

God is not in the business of dispensing curses. In fact, He sent Jesus to redeem us from curses. God does not send calamity our way if we don't love Jesus.

The earth is under the curse of the Fall as a result of Adam's original sin, so many people suffer from that, but God doesn't send that suffering. This earth is cursed, and we're not redeemed from that yet. What we are redeemed from, though, is the curse of the law. (Galatians 3:3) Jesus came to deliver us from that.

What the Bible is saying when it tells us a curse will result from not loving the Lord is that people will end up suffering needlessly from the curse of the fall of Adam if they choose not to love as they should. Therefore, we can't afford not to cultivate love and affection for the Lord. This is our staying power against backsliding.

Our ability to be an affectionate person, first to the Lord and then to other people, is crucially important to your welfare upon this earth. It's vital to develop your capacity to love others emotionally.

Many people have never approached their emotional capacity to love others as something that could be learned. Most people think it's something that just happens—either there's a certain chemistry with someone or there's not and we either like someone or we don't.

Loving others with godly emotions is a learned response. We can cultivate affection for people regardless of the way they treat us.

"Oh, Mac, you don't know how they treated me!" you may say. "They just hate me. How can I possibly feel affection for them?"

We *can* feel affection for people who have hurt us, and we *must* if we're going to operate in the love of God. Walking in love toward others is the only way we'll turn that relationship around, the only way we'll influence that person in a godly way, and the only way we'll simplify our lives.

Therefore, our goal should be to learn to love those who are unkind to us.

In the area of marriage, the Scripture says this: "That they may teach the young women to be sober, to love their husbands, to love their children" (Titus 2:4).

This was written to older women who were encouraged to teach the younger women to feel affection (phileo) for their husbands and their children. Affection can be taught. It is a choice.

You mean it doesn't just happen?

If you've been married more than a day, you know it doesn't just happen. Loving someone with godly affection is learned, and it should be protected and cultivated. It may not come naturally, but it will come if we cultivate and practice it long enough.

God has given us the ability to feel love for other people, so it's vital that we learn how.

At this point men may say to themselves, "But I'm a man, and men don't express affection." It's an out-of-date myth that

somehow a masculine person can't or shouldn't express affection. That misconception should have gone out with bustles
years ago. The point is, we must become an affectionate
person. It's crucial for the health of our most important relationships. That means we may have to change the way we see
ourselves. Maybe we should stop seeing ourselves as hard-
nosed businessmen or really tough individuals. Replace that
image, and instead, try to see yourself as an affectionate and
loving person. Change the inner picture of yourself. Men, it
doesn't have to be a compromise of your manliness; as a matter
of fact, it'll enhance your manliness if you'll do it God's way.
Be open and rely on the Holy Spirit to be your teacher.

The phrase "be sober" in Titus 2:4 means "to be sound-
minded"[1]—in other words, to think clearly and rightly. A
sound-minded person is one who thinks in line with God's
Word. This person casts down thoughts of sin and sickness and
replaces them with thoughts of holiness and health. They
bring every thought captive to the obedience of Christ, cast
down vain imaginations, and think on things that are pure,
lovely, and of a good report. (Philippians 4:8)

As we begin to cultivate godly affection for others, we need
to line up our thinking with what the Word says about them.
Some Scriptures are specific (Ephesians 5:22-28, 6:4), but, in
general, the Word tells us to think about people according to
1 Corinthians 13:7 (Amp.), which says, "Love...is ever ready to
believe the best of every person."

Our emotional response is a product of our thought patterns, and thoughts can change. We can generate any thoughts we choose about other people.

For example, if we began dwelling on how rude and unmannerly certain people treat us, remembering the pain they caused us, we would then cultivate negative feelings toward them.

If, on the other hand, we wanted to cultivate affection for certain people, we might start by thinking about how nice they look or how warm they act. We would think about their love for us. It's easy to love people who love us first. If they're intelligent and sensitive enough to love us in the first place, then they must be worth our love in return!

The Bible encourages us to think about people in a good light. Think about the positive aspects of their personality, and always believe the best about them.

In our society, we're often prompted to do just the opposite. I come in contact with people every day who reflexively believe the worst about people. They don't use sound thinking and often assume others have it in for them. These kinds of people rehearse their relational problems over and over with thoughts like, *The boss doesn't like me. I don't think I'm going to get a raise. I'm never going to measure up.*

But if we obey God's instructions, we'll train ourselves to think optimistically, believing the best about others and ourselves, not the worst. Never forget, "Love hopes all things and believes all things." (1 Corinthians 13:7) Some people might think that's just being naïve—that we're setting ourselves up to get slammed down or hurt. No, that's trusting God by doing it His way. God's Word, like His love, cannot fail. We can make the choice to believe people are going to be a blessing in our lives.

Begin acting as if you believe the best about others and the feelings will follow. Sometimes we have to act in faith and let the feelings follow later. We may not always feel affection for our husband or wife, but we can act that way in faith and the feeling will ultimately come.

SEEDS OF AFFECTION

The Bible tells us that a man's harvest in life depends entirely on what he sows. (Galatians 6:7) So, if you want to be an affectionate person, you must plant seeds of affection. Showing kindness and reverence toward those you esteem will produce results.

Let me tell you a story that illustrates this. My wife has a little Yorkshire terrier named Muffin.

I never have liked little dogs; my wife is the one who likes them. I like big, manly dogs, but she doesn't care for them. She likes little dogs.

We had big dogs when we were first married, but with all the traveling I did, it didn't work out and eventually they had to go. Ever since then, I've wanted big dogs again.

Besides the traveling, we never lived in a house with enough surrounding property to accommodate a big dog. I want the dog to have enough space to run around and enjoy living there. Well, that all changed a few years ago when we decided to buy some property and build a house. Part of the reason for doing this, in my mind, was so that I could get my big dog and let him run around. I also wanted to take him hunting with me.

Because Lynne doesn't like big dogs, we made an agreement and decided to have two dogs—one little dog for her, and, of course, a big one for me.

This made her happy, so she went out and bought a little Yorkshire terrier and brought it home. I took one look at that little dog and thought it was the wimpiest little excuse for a dog I had ever seen. It was a sissy dog! But that was okay because our deal was that I could get my own big dog.

Everything was fine until the deal on the property fell through, and I didn't get my dog. No big dog for me. So now I found myself stuck with a little dog that I had no intention of liking. I must confess, I had a horrible attitude toward that dog. Not only did I not get the property and the big dog I wanted, but now I was stuck with this little dog named, of all things, Muffin!

I wasn't going to like that little dog. I just knew it. In fact, I was going to hate it!

Well, for some reason (it must have been God), little Muffin wouldn't quit loving me. When I came home, she'd jump up to my leg, and I'd push her away. But she never quit loving me. At night when I went to my room, she'd be lying there on the bed like a queen or something, and I'd toss her onto the floor. But she never quit loving me.

When I'd sit down in a chair, she'd jump into my lap, and I'd shove her off. But she never quit loving me.

I was determined not to like that little dog, but she would not quit loving me. It had to be supernatural. I think God was using her to teach me a lesson. She just wouldn't quit. I'm sure you can guess what happened. Muffin loved her way right into my heart. I absolutely couldn't help it. I'm not ashamed to tell you today that I dearly love that little sissy dog.

My point is, when we sow seeds of affection, it establishes a bond of love that will eventually take hold no matter how stubborn people may be. They may hate us with every fiber of their being, but if we keep finding ways to express love to them, making gestures of affection and kindness, eventually a bond of affection will develop. And when it does, God will have a relationship He can use to pour blessings through.

We can exercise more godly influence over others than we ever dreamed possible. As we sow seeds of love, we'll reap a harvest of rich relationships and a blessed, simplified life.

PRACTICE PRAYING FOR OTHERS

Another way to cultivate godly affection for people is to start praying for them. When we pray for people on a continual basis, we cannot help but learn to like them. It's virtually impossible to dislike someone we're investing prayer time and energy into.

Praying for people we want to form relationships with is the most significant form of giving we can do for them. There's nothing you can give that has greater significance or potential for change than consistent, fervent prayer.

As you know, wherever you put your treasure, there your heart will be also. (Matthew 6:21) It's the principle of giving and receiving. We cannot give prayer for another person and not experience a heart change ourselves.

I know this firsthand. A few years ago, a certain individual really came against this ministry and me personally. So I started praying for that person in this manner.

For a while, my prayers were simply a matter of discipline, effort, and faith. I had to pray for this person in faith because I didn't have the feelings to back up my prayers. At first, it was just a matter of doing what the Word said. I prayed for this person who despitefully used me. (Luke 6:28)

Ultimately though, God began doing a work in me. He began showing me how He saw this individual. I began to see this person through the eyes of the Lord, and it changed the way I felt. I began to have compassion and pity on him as I continued to pray.

You see, it doesn't matter how badly people act toward us. When we see them the way God sees them—that they're precious enough for Him to send Jesus to die for them—we begin to see beyond the way they've treated us. We can see that things going on in their lives may be contributing to their behavior. There may even be demonic warfare coming against them that we can't see unless we pray for them. Perhaps Satan is influencing them in such a way that they're tormented inside. Praying for them generates awareness and compassion in us.

We'll begin to see them as God sees them—precious and valuable even though deceived and hurting. As we pray for them, we can ask God to bring about a mighty change in the relationship, and He'll do it.

When we begin controlling our thought lives, thinking the best and believing the best about people, sowing seeds of affection into their lives, our actions will begin to bring about some mighty changes. Rough relationships will begin to smooth over.

Others might not change as dramatically, but we certainly will. It's all part of properly managing your relationships.

When we manage relationships properly, they'll become a blessing to us instead of a curse. Contention and jealousy will depart, life will become simpler. We'll also open other channels of blessing through which God can minister to us.

It's a lesson we all would do well to learn. The love of God plays such a vital part in our lives, and we need more of it. Embracing godly love will enable us to give more agape and phileo love to others. As we learn to sustain agape love and phileo love, the feelings of affection will follow. Together, we will have the capacity to properly manage our relationships while improving the quality of our own lives.

FOURTEEN

UNDERSTANDING AUTHORITY

Since Jesus commands us to let our light shine and to be the salt of the earth, He wants us to exercise godly influence in the lives of those He brings to us. I believe that's the ultimate reason we are to manage our relationships well. Doing this will simplify our lives.

There is also a very strong personal benefit for us when we build and cultivate godly relationships. God will use healthy relationships as channels of blessing, encouragement, direction, and provision in our own lives. Of course, all that we do to serve others should be motivated by love.

When we walk in love toward others, our relationships will be fruitful and we can avoid unnecessary schisms, divisions, and contentions between others and ourselves.

The one common denominator that always applies to every relationship is to love others with the love of God. God's love compels us to serve others (Mark 9:35), but that doesn't mean we have to somehow become another person's slave. The biblical definition for serving others simply means to assist or to help someone. To serve is to provide another person with something they need or desire. That's all serving means.

As a matter of fact, the primary word defined as "to serve" in the New Testament is *diakoneo*. This word means "to minister."[1] So remove from your thinking the idea of being in captivity to someone else. That's not what this concept means at all.

Jesus served others, and He certainly wasn't a slave. We see Jesus laying down His deity and taking on the form of a servant in the days of His earthly ministry (Philippians 2:7), and we are to be conformed to His image. So, we need to develop a servant's heart. If Jesus took on the form of a servant when responding to God's love, then we should model our actions after this same manner and conduct our relationships on the basis of that same love. That means we should be willing to serve other people.

THREE CLASSES OF RELATIONSHIPS

We can identify three basic classes of relationships as found in the Word of God. Even though love or service is the common denominator among them, we respond to each one differently. Lines of authority determine these classes.

The first class is peer relationships. These include our friends or anyone who is our equal in matters of authority. The other two classes are those to whom we submit and those who submit to us.

If we want our relationships to be healthy and to be a blessing to us, we will want to learn how to manage them well. To succeed in that, we need to recognize each class of relationships and then learn to manage them according to relevant godly principles.

We can't manage all three classes of relationships in the same way. Yes, the common denominator, God's love, must be at the heart of all interactions, but there are specific ways in which to manage each type of relationship. If we try to approach each one the same way, we're going to have problems.

MANAGING PEER RELATIONSHIPS

Let's begin by looking at our relationships with peers. The Bible says, "Let us consider one another to provoke unto love and to good works: not forsaking the assembling of ourselves together" (Hebrews 10:24,25). The Greek word translated as *assembling* refers to a meaningful piecing together of parts that form a whole, not to a haphazard gathering of people. God has placed every member in the body into the role that pleases Him. (1 Corinthians 12:18)

There's a place for each of us in the body of Christ. Like a piece in a jigsaw puzzle, there is a place where we fit into God's plan. It's not a haphazard thing; we fit into the place where God has assigned us.

We're instructed to love, minister to, and serve other believers. Furthermore, we know that we gain contact to our peers by virtue of the position in which God has assigned us within the body of Christ.

The Amplified translation says this:

*And let us consider and give attentive, continuous care to
watching over one another, studying how we may stir up (stimu-
late and incite) to love and helpful deeds and noble activities.*

Hebrews 10:24 Amp.

People in the world tend to say, "Stay out of my business
and I'll stay out of yours," but God wants us to minister to the
needs of our peers in love, giving them care and attention that
only comes when we have a healthy relationship with them.

As believers we are to pursue active relationships with our
fellow Christians, holding them accountable to godliness and
serving them in love. God wants us to be aware of needs other
believers may have in order to minister to, serve, and encourage them in the Lord.

But what about serving non-Christian peers, such as the
people in our neighborhood or at work? How do you manage
those kinds of relationships?

In my opinion, we can approach our relationships with
unbelievers solely on the basis of sharing Jesus with them.
Other than that common issue, we should not have intimate
fellowship with unbelievers.

That doesn't mean we should burn the bridges of relationships we may have already formed with non-Christians. To be
in fellowship with someone means to share from your heart
with him or her. The Bible teaches that there is to be no
fellowship—or the sharing of the heart—between a believer
and an unbeliever.

Many of us have the idea that we're going to infect all of our unbelieving acquaintances with our holiness the minute we come into contact with them. But God makes it clear that holiness is not infectious. Instead, unholiness is infectious. If we maintain fellowship with an unbeliever, we will most likely be the ones to be infected with unholiness. That's why God says light should have no fellowship with darkness. (2 Corinthians 6:14) So, the only basis on which to relate to an unbeliever is that of sharing Jesus.

Now, that doesn't necessarily mean we just walk up to somebody and figuratively slap him across the cheek and tell him that he needs to be saved. Confrontational evangelism is something to which some people may be called, but most of us aren't. Instead, wait for God to give you a door of opportunity to minister Jesus to an individual.

We can also find opportunities to minister Jesus to nonbelievers by serving them in the physical, seemingly non-spiritual realm. This is the point where providing for someone's natural or physical needs becomes important. Ultimately, you can't totally serve human needs without serving them Jesus and the Word of God. Often the door to a nonbeliever's heart is not open to receive any kind of ministry except through natural means.

That's exactly what Jesus did in the Bible. He met natural human needs when He fed the five thousand after they had followed Him around for three days. (Matthew 14:18-21) In order to minister the Word of God to them, He first fed them.

The same will be true for us. If we have neighbors with whom we want to share Jesus, the best way to find an opportunity might be to bake them a pan of muffins or cut their grass when they are on vacation. Look for ways to serve their needs and share Jesus.

I'm reminded of a pastor who once started a church in a northern climate where it snowed often. Initially, his church was small; just a few people were coming. But he had a truck with a snowplow on the front that he used for clearing the small parking lot at church.

During one snowy day, he decided to plow the driveways of all of his neighbors, in addition to the church parking lot. He plowed their driveways and left a card in their garage doors, telling them: "Jesus loves you. Come and see some nice folks at church sometime."

Let me tell you something, friend. Up north if you plow somebody's driveway after a snowstorm, you've done something worth receiving love and appreciation for. That opens people's hearts! And it did for this man's neighbors.

His church membership increased tremendously just by his having plowed everybody's driveway. He got their attention by loving them and serving them in the natural, and ultimately it opened their hearts to the Gospel. As a result, many of his neighbors received the Lord.

That's the way to manage non-Christian relationships with your peers. Serve them, share the Gospel, and be the one to influence them for good.

SUBMITTING TO AUTHORITY

By far, the most important and significant relationships we will have in our lives are those in which we are either submitting to authority or others are submitting to our authority.

These relationships are so important because that's where we can wield the most influence and have the greatest opportunity to impact somebody else's life.

Relationships involving authority are designed to bring direction to the body of Christ. These relationships are probably the most challenging and require the greatest management effort, but the rewards are also usually the greatest.

Lines of authority within relationships prevent anarchy and chaos. God is not a God of anarchy, and He's not a God of chaos or confusion. He brought order and creation out of chaos, and He designed relationships to be the same way. Order cannot exist without the proper authority being in place. God has ordained the structure of authority as part of the human experience.

Actually, there are different kinds of authority set into place in this world. For example, there's parental authority, spiritual authority, vocational authority, civil authority, and even governmental authority on a variety of levels.

Authority touches our lives in virtually every spectrum of human endeavor and experience. It is the plan from which God brings order, direction, cohesion of effort, and group or corporate productivity. Without authority, none of these things would happen.

The Bible has a lot to say about authority. For example, look at Romans 13:1. "Let every soul be subject unto [submitted to] the higher powers." Notice that it says, "every soul." There are no exclusions made in this statement.

The Greek word translated as *power* in this verse is *exousia*, and it literally means "authority."[2] As a matter of fact, most translations use the word *authority* instead of *power*.

This verse could be accurately read by using the words *authority* and *power* interchangeably. Doing so makes its true meaning clearer. For example, "Let every soul be subject or be submitted unto the higher *authorities*." It's plural, and it means God's talking about every office of authority. "For there is no *authority* but of God: the *authorities* that be are ordained of God." (Romans 13:1)

To properly understand authority, it is vital to make a distinction between the *office* of authority and the *person* who fills that particular office.

People may decide the office of authority needs to be ignored because the person in charge is corrupt, abusive, or irresponsible. We can all think of people who stood in offices of authority who, through either incompetence or maliciousness, fostered a tremendous amount of human suffering. Many dictators did this very thing.

But God does not say that only *some* offices of authority need to be respected, depending on the man who stands in them. No, God says He's ordained *every* office of authority. And we will be successful only to the degree we learn to relate to those offices of authority properly.

Frankly, God can use anyone to bring blessing to our lives. That's why we have to become skilled at responding properly to the offices of authority that touch our lives, regardless of the attributes of the people who stand in them.

Did you know that if we do our part and relate properly to an office of authority, God could still bless us even though the person in that office may be evil, corrupt, or even demon-possessed? There are examples of this in the Bible.

For example, it happened during the reign of an evil king named Cyrus. Even though he was an evil king, God used him to initiate the rebuilding of Jerusalem and to promote the plan of God. (Ezra 5:13)

It doesn't matter who stands in an office of authority; we still must respect it. When in comes to political authority, it doesn't matter if you're a Democrat or a Republican. It doesn't matter if you voted for him or her, like him or her, or agree with his or her policies. The Bible says we must respect the office, and if we do, God can bring blessing to us through it.

For wives, the most important thing to understand is the office your husband holds as head of the household. He may be ungodly or unsaved; however, God's desire is that you respect his position of authority. He may be difficult to live with and nowhere close to serving God. However, by respecting your husband's office of authority, God will bless you, and by your godly actions, God can change your husband if he chooses to yield to the power of the Holy Spirit.

There is no *office* of authority that has not been established by God. Satan never created an office of authority, but he may

199

try to corrupt the person who stands in it in order to promote his own purposes. He's behind all rebellion, anarchy, and chaos.

Too many Christians have the idea that to be liberated in Christ means to be liberated from accountability to authority. This is a deadly fallacy.

As I've said, spiritually there's a difference between the individual in authority and the office. We must learn to respect the office of authority, whether it be the office of husband, supervisor, city councilman, policeman, or President of the United States. We have no right to disrespect any office of authority.

God's Word says, "Whosoever therefore resisteth the power [authority], resisteth the ordinance of God: and they that resist shall receive to themselves damnation" (Romans 13:2). Resisting authority is not the way to go about promoting change.

Our understanding of this principle is extremely important, because many people in our nation have lost that kind of respect for authority. In a lot of ways, we've become a rebellious nation.

We've condoned all sorts of things that violate the ordinances of God by rejecting the office of authority God put into place for our benefit.

The consequences of this kind of behavior are not good.

For rulers are not a terror to good works, but to the evil. Wilt thou then not be afraid of the power? do that which is good, and thou shalt have praise of the same.

Romans 13:3

200

God's Word doesn't make any distinction about which rulers we're to respect. There have been a lot of bad rulers whom God nevertheless expected us to respect—because of their position of authority.

This brings to the forefront the subject of obedience. We can't talk about authority without talking about obedience. If we are submitting to a body of authority, whether it be the spiritual authority in the home, the civil authority in government, or the vocational authority at the workplace, the final measurement of obedience has to be to the Word of God.

There is only one thing we are told to obey without question, and that's the Bible. Questions of authority must always be measured against the Word of God.

Paul said, "Follow after me as I follow after Christ." (1 Corinthians 11:1) He didn't tell people to blindly follow him no matter what he did. No, Paul told them follow after him as he followed after Christ. So, all authority should first pass the test of the Word of God. For example, a man's wife should not go to a bar with him in the name of being submissive. That's sin because it goes against the Word. And a man has no authority to keep his wife from going to church or from worshiping God.

The laws of God that run contrary to the laws of the land should take precedence in our lives. Regardless of what the laws of the land say, abortion is not something we should ever engage in. God says it's not right to take innocent life. Therefore, when the law of God runs contrary to civil law or to authority in general and the personal life of a believer is infringed upon, we always go with the law of God. Authority is designed to govern group issues, and only to a lesser degree, individual matters. We have the Holy Spirit to govern the affairs of our personal life. All we have to do is ask God for specific direction and then follow His will, which always brings peace.

Don't let others direct the personal matters of your life under the guise of being in authority over you. However, where group matters are concerned, remember that God establishes authority to bring direction and cohesion to them.

This isn't to suggest that some people are better than others. On the contrary, we're all equal in Christ. (Galatians 3:26) God's not saying that because the wife isn't the final decision-maker in the marriage relationship she's somehow inferior to her husband. We're all equal in Christ, and we're to submit to each other in love. (Ephesians 5:21)

Someone, however, has to ultimately be responsible or anarchy and chaos will result, no matter what size group it is.

Some people hear this kind of teaching and say to themselves, *Well, I've got the Holy Spirit on the inside, so I don't need to listen to what anyone else tells me to do.* They may even back up this kind of rationale by quoting a Scripture such as, "But ye have an unction from the Holy One, and ye know all things" (1 John 2:20).

This Scripture has often been abused to rationalize an unteachable nature in some.

Think about it. Why did God ordain ministry in the first place if we didn't need to be taught things? Clearly, we need to remain teachable, and the Holy Spirit is there to help us. The Word makes it clear that the Holy Spirit guides us into all truth. (John 16:13) That's why we don't need somebody to come up and prophesy over us to tell us things such as when it's time to get married. If you don't know that on your own, then you've got a real problem.

We know "all things" because the Holy Spirit teaches us. That's why we don't need some flaky person to prophesy and tell us to give away all our money to his or her ministry. We should know these types of things on our own.

But that doesn't mean we don't need authority in our life— far from it.

SUBMITTING TO
ONE ANOTHER IN LOVE

The authority of the Holy Spirit governs our heart and conscience, and He will help us exercise authority over those who submit to us. This is even true in the marriage relationship.

Submitting yourselves one to another in the fear of God. Wives, submit yourselves unto your own husbands, as unto the Lord. For the husband is the head of the wife, even as Christ is the head of the church: and he is the saviour of the body. Therefore as the church is subject unto Christ, so let the wives be to their own husbands in every thing. Husbands, love your wives, even as Christ also loved the church, and gave himself for it; that

203

he might sanctify and cleanse it with the washing of water by the
word, that he might present it to himself a glorious church, not
having spot, or wrinkle, or any such thing; but that it should be
holy and without blemish. So ought men to love their wives as
their own bodies. He that loveth his wife loveth himself.

Ephesians 5:21-28

By far, one of the most important relationships involving godly authority is the relationship between husband and wife. The Bible compares the marriage relationship to that between Jesus Christ and the Church.

Christ's relationship with the Church sets the pattern for all other relationships to follow, including husbands to wives, children to parents, employees to employers, and so on.

Let me stress again that submission does not mean blind obedience. Submission recognizes the need for authority in order to avoid chaos while bringing meaning and direction to a particular group. We should measure any direction given by the standard of God's Word before we decide whether to not to obey it.

The husband is the head of the wife, even as Christ is the head of the Church. Therefore, as the Church is subject under Christ, so let the wives be subject to their own husbands in the same pattern of submission to authority.

And husbands, God turns that around and tells you that you must love your wife as Christ loves the Church. (Ephesians 5:25) And let me tell you how important that is. In order for the smooth pattern of submission and authority to work between husbands and wives, there must be love. The only thing that's going to make this principle of authority stay on track is to love each other with the love of God.

Any office that tries to exercise its authority solely on the strength of its position will ultimately fail. Most of the secular world runs on the strength of positional authority. The military, for example, operates on the principle of fear and strength of position. A lieutenant had better salute the captain, and the captain had better salute the major, and so on. Because in the military, as in other secular bodies of authority, rank determines authority.

Adherence to positional authority is the way much of the world runs. Positional authority asserts, "I'm the boss! You do what I say." But enforced submission produces one of two results—bondage and servitude or rebellion.

The only way submission to authority works the way the Bible intends is when the person who is submitting does so willingly and from the heart. This can happen only when he or she is confident that the person in authority walks in love and is keeping his or her best interests at heart.

So, if you are in authority over others, remember to exercise authority according to the standard of God's Word, applying that standard of love toward the people you manage. Love them. Serve them.

As leaders, we should serve others by asking ourselves, "What's best for my wife or for my children? What can I do to best serve the interests of those who are accountable to me?" We should treat others as we would treat ourselves. When we do this, we will ultimately take care of our own best interests as well.

So, if you're an entrepreneur managing hundreds of people, resist being motivated exclusively by the bottom line. Your motive shouldn't be to make as much money as possible or to elevate your status in the business arena at any cost. You have an obligation to serve those who serve under your authority rather than exploit them.

This idea may be a major paradigm shift for those of us in industry and the business community, but if this philosophy were adopted, we would see that we would actually be serving the best interests of our companies and the stockholders. If business leaders truly understood the biblical truth that states those who want to be the chief of all need to be the servant of all (Luke 22:26), that knowledge would change the world.

If leaders could adopt this attitude, there would be no need for labor unions or contract negotiations or labor strikes. Instead, employees could receive direction from the godly business leader's example, promoting unity, harmony, and concord of purpose that cannot be matched in the secular world.

That is what it is all about. Serving those whom God has entrusted to our care is our primary responsibility. Of course, we need to be financially responsible—the bottom line does matter, but we should not be managing with the idea of laying off as many people as we can just to turn a bigger buck. If things get a little financially tight in your business, it is my opinion that your first obligation is to serve the interests of your employees. Ask the Holy Spirit to give you creative ways to keep people on payroll and work things out somehow so that you can be a blessing to them.

This principle of serving others and treating them like you want to be treated also applies to us when we are under authority. We are to respect that unsaved, cranky supervisor we might work for—not because he or she is worthy of it any more than we're worthy of it—but because God has ordained the office.

The Bible tells us to pray for those in positions of authority. It doesn't matter who the person is, or whether or not we agree with their theological or political viewpoint. We are nevertheless called to pray earnestly for those we serve.

Servants, be obedient to them that are your masters according to the flesh, with fear and trembling, in singleness of your heart, as unto Christ; not with eyeservice, as menpleasers; but as the servants of Christ, doing the will of God from the heart; with good will doing service, as to the Lord, and not to men.

Ephesians 6:5-7

Wherever you work, give 100 percent effort to the job. I suggest you get to work early and work hard at your job, whether you think your boss deserves it or not. Give him or her all you can give, not to be "men pleasers" as the Bible puts it, but because you're working as unto the Lord.

The Bible makes it clear that we're not to manipulate people. Ephesians 6:9 says, "And, ye masters, do the same things unto them, forbearing threatening: knowing that your Master also is in heaven; neither is there respect of persons with him." In other words, don't use threats or intimidation with your boss or your family. Don't threaten your employees with the possibility of a demotion or a salary reduction if they don't perform well. Likewise, don't threaten to zap your kids if they don't do their chores. Refuse to use threats or intimidation in general.

On the other hand, discipline is necessary and appropriate in certain instances. For example, the Bible tells us to use the rod with our children when necessary to correct them. (Proverbs 22:15) Also, part of the responsibility as a leader involves exercising authority to train and discipline those under us. However, under normal circumstances, in the day-to-day general conduct with others, we are to "forbear threatening."

Using threats or intimidation will never produce godly results. Rather, it is the use of love and goodness that will produce that. Notice what the Bible has to say about this: "Likewise, ye wives, be in subjection to your own husbands; that, if any obey not the word, they also may without the word be won by the conversation [manner of life] of the wives" (1 Peter 3:1).

Now, don't preach to your unsaved spouse, employee, supervisor, manager, or boss. In general, don't preach at others. Notice, I didn't say, "Don't witness." I said, "Don't preach." There is a difference.

Our lifestyle should be our witness of God's goodness and truth. He can do more to change the lives of those in authority around us when we simply live by the standard of His Word, upholding godly values and biblical principles, than when we "preach." When we combine the virtues of hard work and godly values in the workplace, our bosses will notice. We won't have to preach; our lifestyle will witness for us and we'll become the most valuable person to the organization, the best wife to any husband, or the best husband to any wife.

More change came to my life, especially when I wasn't walking with the Lord as I should have been, just by observing the manner of my wife's life. I watched how she related to me as a wife. She was determined to minister to me and to be a better wife to me than ever before. She used the standard of God's Word to change her life more than any other single factor. And it worked! In fact, I attribute my response to the ministry call directly to her actions during that time in my life.

SUBMISSION TO AUTHORITY

Every one of us is accountable to someone else's authority in one way or another. So, we need to be mindful of what it takes to be a steward of these relationships. The following five scriptural guidelines are a summary of what we've already covered, and they will help us manage these relationships better as we incorporate the principles into our lives.

1. Let every soul be submitted to authority.

(Romans 13:1)

We must recognize that the office of authority, regardless of the person standing in it, is ordained of God.

2. Servants, be obedient to them. (Ephesians 6:5)

We as Christians must obey the direction or instruction that comes from an office of authority. Of course, we must measure everything against the standard of the Word. Submitting to authority does not mean we blindly obey what someone tells us to do when it contradicts God's Word.

3. Serve as unto the Lord and not unto men.

(Ephesians 6:7)

We need to do our very best to contribute to the corporate effort by making an effort to give 100 percent. But we need to work as unto the Lord. Arrive early and work hard—not to please man, but to please the Lord. And, in return, we'll be blessed when we do.

4. Let your light shine. (Matthew 5:16)

Don't preach or lecture to that unsanctified husband or wife, and don't preach to that unsaved boss. The Bible tells us that if we live our lives by the standard of God's Word, God can change the life of an unbeliever. Our *lifestyles,* lived according to the standard of the Word, will convict another person of sin.

5. Pray for those in authority. (1 Timothy 2:1,2)

The Bible tells us to pray for those in positions of authority. It doesn't matter who the person is or whether or not we agree with his or her theological or political viewpoint. We are nevertheless called to pray earnestly for those we serve.

The Bible commands us to respect, honor, and esteem that office of authority because God ordained it, and when we line ourselves up with it, we'll be blessed.

EXERCISING AUTHORITY

Now, let's review God's principles for relating to those in authority. When it comes to others who are accountable to us—whether it's a child, spouse, or colleague—we must manage those relationships well in order to exercise the greatest degree of godly influence possible.

As I've said already, this is a very different dynamic than that of relating to those to whom we are submitted. As we look to the Word, we find four keys to managing this type of relationship.

1. He who wishes to be great must be a servant. (Mark 9:34,35)

As someone holding a position of authority, our primary motive should be to serve those under that authority. Although this may run opposite to what most other people in authority do, you will find that serving others is the most effective way to manage.

2. The greatest of these is love. (1 Corinthians 13:13)

Instead of mistreating those under our authority, treat them with affectionate care and attention, loving them according to the Word of God. Authority only works when submission is willing and from the heart. There's only one thing that makes that happen, and that's to love people as Christ loved the Church. (Ephesians 5:25)

3. Provoke not your children to wrath. (Ephesians 6:4)

As we manage relationships, don't provoke people under you to wrath by threatening and intimidating them. It'll only generate anger and hostility. Walls will go up, and division and mistrust will follow. Instead, admonish or exhort them with affectionate care and attention.

4. Train up a child. (Proverbs 22:6)

A major part of our authoritative responsibility is to train those under our care. God expects us to cultivate His gifts within them and help them grow into their call in life.

So, whether we're talking about our children, our spouse, or someone under our authority in the workplace, becoming a better manager of our relationships will have great benefits. We will not only increase our own ability to become servants, but we will also increase our ability to influence others to develop the call of God on their life.

This is the reason relationship management is so important. As managers over the relationships God gives to us, we have the awesome responsibility to help people cultivate their God-given gifts and talents and grow and mature in godliness.

We have a responsibility to serve others and initiate the training process. Helping others is the most rewarding job we could ever have, and when we do it right, we will not only improve the quality of our own life, but we will also reap rewards from God for acting in obedience to His will. We *can* make a difference.

One man, Jesus Christ, was so influential in His day that His reputation spread throughout the world. And although He was crucified, His death and resurrection opened the way for us to influence the world with that same love.

FIFTEEN

RESOLVING INTERPERSONAL CONFLICT

We've seen that by becoming better managers of life's primary resources, we can lead a more simplified life. We placed those resources into categories of time, money, and relationships, asserting that if any of these categories are neglected or mismanaged, it can present problems that will complicate life. The solution is to become better managers. Better management allows us to gain access to the light and understanding that the Word of God brings.

We can do everything else right in our lives, but if we get too busy and encumbered (as Martha did in Jesus' time), it is possible to experience the very presence of Jesus Christ Himself without being changed. This problem can be solved by simplifying our lives.

It would be inappropriate to talk about managing relationships without discussing how to restore those that have been damaged through mismanagement.

From time to time, all of us have mismanaged relationships in our lives. We probably didn't mean to do harm to any of them, but perhaps through neglect or lack of attention, we've inadvertently allowed some relationships to taper off. We've all done this at one time or another, but the key is, as the Holy Spirit leads us, to make every effort to restore relationships that have been mismanaged.

A key indicator that a relationship has been mismanaged is to note the presence of conflict, schism, or division. So, how do we resolve the problem?

It is clearly not part of God's perfect will that we live with damaged relationships. God can use well-managed relationships to bring blessing and provision to us. But in the case of mismanaged relationships in which conflict and schisms have occurred, Satan will try to bring the effects of the curse to us instead of blessing. We cannot afford to leave the door open to the enemy.

We have to take positive, proactive steps to ensure that our relationships are running smoothly, and, if they're not, work to restore them. We need to become skilled at resolving interpersonal conflict or Satan will continually have access to harass, distract, and attempt to lower the quality of our lives.

Becoming skilled at conflict resolution involves four primary steps: prayer, forgiveness, communication, and negotiation.

We must use all of these ingredients together, not just one or another separately. We have to give attention to each ingredient for the conflict to be resolved. We can't use prayer alone to restore a mismanaged relationship. Even though without prayer, the resolution of conflict is impossible; prayer alone won't solve the problem. Just using forgiveness to solve our interpersonal problems won't entirely fix them either.

So if we concentrate only on prayer, or even on prayer and forgiveness together, we won't make it to the restoration phase of that relationship.

Communication has to be part of the healing process as well. It is impossible to restore a relationship without communicating with the other person involved. We must be able to communicate effectively.

Then we must recognize the need for negotiation. Negotiation is a crucial part of the communication process, and it's a skill used to reach resolution on points of conflict. We must become good negotiators, or we may end up with many unresolved interpersonal conflicts.

Do not confuse negotiation with compromise. They are not the same thing. To negotiate something does not mean we compromise our values or the direction God has given us. Negotiation is a process of communicating that produces a resolution to the conflict.

But conflict resolution begins with prayer. Prayer lays the groundwork for resolving conflict. The Bible commands us to pray for people in general, but we are specifically instructed to pray for those who despitefully use or persecute us. This means we need to pray for those relationships that have developed conflicts or divisions.

Jesus said, "I say unto you, Love your enemies, bless them that curse you, do good to them that hate you, and pray for them which despitefully use you, and persecute you" (Matthew 5:44).

If you're a child of God, you don't have a choice but to pray for others. It's opposite to the way the world practices, but it's a mandate to God's children.

Praying for people who despitefully use us basically does two things. It keeps our heart right toward that person, and it pushes the darkness back from their life.

Now, first of all, we need to keep our heart right toward those who despitefully use us or we won't be able to forgive them. Through prayer, God gives us a healthy perspective of the conflict.

Sometimes it takes a whole lot of prayer to look at people through God's eyes, but it can happen. Ask God to show you the way He sees them, and before long, you won't be able to continue harboring the bitterness or resentment that would otherwise be there.

Prayer helps to restore those divided relationships and provides us an opportunity to make healthy decisions about them.

When a relationship is divided, it can mean there are demonic influences at work. It could also be just the nature of the flesh, but sometimes demonic forces will try to influence us to allow ourselves to become hurt or offended. Satan tries to impose his will on the lives of believers, but we don't have to let him.

When we pray for others, we can't impose our will on them through prayer. God doesn't allow that. He doesn't even impose Himself on others. But by praying, we can stop Satan from sabotaging our relationships and then God can change them.

Prayer moves the hand of the enemy back. It keeps the darkness at bay so we can see things clearly and make healthy decisions. Then, once we've begun seeing things from a godly perspective, it's easier to forgive because now we're motivated to do so.

Forgiveness is the second ingredient required to restore divided relationships. Actually, God commands us to forgive others whether we feel like it or not, but it's a lot easier to forgive after preparing our hearts with prayer.

I've heard people say, "I can't forgive them. You don't know how badly they abused me. You don't know what my past was like. It's impossible for me to forgive what they did to me."

Our spiritual life depends upon forgiving others, no matter what they did to us. God doesn't say, "Forgive if you can." He commands us to forgive, period. As a matter of fact, Mark 11:25 says that God's willingness to forgive us depends on our willingness to forgive others. Unforgiveness hurts us far more than it hurts the other person.

We must forgive and forget, no matter how hard it may be. We can't forgive someone and then keep bringing the hurt back up in our memory every time we think about that person. That's not true forgiveness.

Once again, I encounter people all the time who say they've forgiven someone, but then they tell me every detail of exactly how wronged they were. They haven't truly forgiven. If those injustices are still a dominant part of their thought life, then they haven't truly forgiven at all.

God said He's removed our sin as far as the east is from the west. (Psalms 103:12) He remembers them no more. That is our pattern for forgiving others. We have the ability to choose which thoughts we will think and which ones we won't. If the enemy tries to bring to your remembrance how badly you were treated, refuse to entertain it. Instead, bring those thoughts captive into the obedience of Christ. (2 Corinthians 10:5) Cast down those vain imaginations and thoughts. Forget in order to forgive. Aren't you glad God forgot what you used to be like?

I don't care how many times we have to mouth the words, "I forgive you," or "God, I forgive them." If it's still a dominant part of our thought life, we haven't truly forgiven them. And that indicates a broken relationship that will complicate our lives and hold us back spiritually and materially.

Sometimes we even maintain double standards on the subject of forgiveness. We may say, for example, "Thank You, God, for erasing my past," while we keep another person's past continually before them. That is unforgiveness, and it requires prayer. Prayer is the first ingredient toward relationship restoration, and forgiveness comes next.

Maybe you're the one who's caused someone else to stumble. Forgiveness works both ways. If you've done something that has offended someone else, you need to go and ask that person to forgive you. The Word says, "Go to your brother and be reconciled with him" (Matthew 5:24). In other words, when someone has ought against you, you need to go to him or her and say, "I'm sorry. Let's get this straightened out." We need to be reconciled to that brother or sister who harbors unforgiveness toward us. Divisions between believers are not acceptable before God.

Then the third thing we need to do to restore a broken relationship is to open up the channels of communication. We need to talk to the person in question. Sometimes, that's exactly the opposite of what we want to do. It's just human nature. When conflict arises between us and somebody else, the first thing many of us want to do is retire into our self-righteous shell and say nothing to him.

"How could he be so stupid!" we might say. We all do that sometimes, don't we?

We all face the same challenges where our human nature is concerned. Our tendency is to withdraw when conflict arises. But if we're going to resolve it, we must communicate. We have to talk to that person in love.

To communicate is to literally exchange information. However, when most people are upset over interpersonal conflicts, they may want to communicate by simply giving the other person a piece of their mind. Clearly, that's not godly communication.

One of Stephen Covey's famous seven habits of highly effective people is this: "Seek first to understand, then to be understood."[1]

True communication is an *exchange* of information, and it means that the other person gets a say in things too. So, communication between two people who are resolving a conflict must be equal for it to be productive. There's a difference between good communication and bad communication.

Good communication, according to the Bible, produces edification and ministers grace to the hearer. (Ephesians 4:29)

The Bible also talks about corrupt communication, which it defines as evil speaking, bitterness, clamor, wrath, and anger. (Ephesians 4:29-31) Obviously, this is the wrong way to communicate, and it should be avoided. Instead of going to someone in anger or wrath, wait until you calm down and go to him or her in love and sympathy, determined in your heart to see his or her point of view. Work things out and talk about it, then move on and commit it to God. Forgive, then forget.

Communication skills are vitally important to every area of our lives. We could be a dynamic, anointed leader with a vision for changing the world, but if we can't communicate that vision, nobody will follow us. Likewise, we could be a lover of God and people, with a godly, fervent love and compassion that could transform relationships, but if we can't communicate that love, then it's useless.

Good communication skills are vital in every area of life, so what can make us good communicators?

The Bible says, "Wherefore my beloved brethren, let every man be swift to hear, slow to speak, slow to wrath" (James 1:19). Now, I know a lot of people who have that backward—they're quick to anger, quick to speak, and really slow to listen.

Sometimes we get so busy making our own point that we seldom give time to hearing what the other person is saying. That's not only wrong, but it's extremely counterproductive in resolving conflict. God wants us to learn communication skills that will start us on the road to conflict resolution.

The principles of good communication can, first of all, be viewed as a scriptural guide to avoiding conflicts. But, second, if conflict has arisen, being a good negotiator is a path to resolve the conflict.

Becoming a good negotiator involves several things, but first and foremost, it requires us to be swift to hear. The best communicator is the best listener. Don't let that truth slip by you. We can't possibly have a meaningful exchange of information without listening to the other person. The Word of God asserts over and over that he who has an ear to hear, let him hear. (Revelation 2:7)

God wants us to be good listeners because He has a lot to say to us through the Holy Spirit. One of the ways the Holy Spirit speaks to us is through other people, and we have to have good listening ears to hear what He has to say.

It's difficult to hear His still, small voice if we're swift to speak and slow to hear. One way to prevent this from happening is to remain silent until we've engaged our brain. This may not sound like a deep revelation from God, but it works. Holding our tongues until we've had time to think about what we want to say will help us deal with anger.

Anger is deadly to conflict resolution. That's why one of the first skills that has to be developed when restoring broken relationships is anger management. It is vital that we learn to manage our anger, or we'll never resolve the conflict. This is one of the reasons the Bible tells us not to speak right away. In a heated debate, what might start out as a strong conviction can end up as an emotionally volatile argument. Anger sets in, and the negotiation process breaks down.

Okay, so you've got your anger under control, but the other guy can't control his. Well, the book of Proverbs gives us the solution by stating that a soft answer turns away wrath. (Proverbs 15:1)

We can always pop somebody's anger balloon with a soft answer. And, in the meantime, it's really a fun thing to do. The Word always works. Anger will always diminish with the exchange of a soft answer.

There was a time some years ago when we got involved in an inner-city outreach, distributing food and clothing to the less fortunate. It was originally located in a rough part of the city in an old, converted saloon. That bar had historically been one of those places downtown where the police were called out on nearly a nightly basis. It was a rough area.

Our church got involved in an effort to move God into the community and move Satan out. It was a step in the right direction, and I thought surely the community would open their arms to us and embrace it gladly. Who wouldn't want a benevolent Christian outreach there instead of a crime- and violence-infested magnet for shady characters?

Well, I soon found out. The community organized a town hall meeting and invited our church to attend as a new member of the inner-city community. But little did I know they were laying-in-wait for me. I naively expected everyone to embrace the fact that we were bringing God into the heart of our city and chasing Satan out. I was wrong.

I quickly learned the meaning of being spiritually tarred, feathered, and run out on a rail. There were four hundred people there, and they had been worked into a lather over the fear that we were going to draw transients and undesirable people into the community by offering free food and clothing to them. They thought we were going to bring every derelict in the city into their neighborhood and further degrade their quality of life.

So when I saw their anger, my first instinct was to get defensive. I started out by saying, "Now, wait a minute...." Contrary to the Word, I wasn't very slow to speak. In fact, I was very quick to defend myself, saying, "No! You don't understand. We're not going to just hand out food to everybody. We're going to invite them to come in and listen to the preaching of the Word. And if they'll make a commitment to get things turned around and become a contributing part of society again, we'll give them more."

They wouldn't hear a word I said. They were so mad and so angry that the more I tried to talk, the less they would hear. They were cursing at me and creating all kinds of negative publicity. The TV cameras were there recording all of it for the evening news!

Finally, the Holy Spirit got through to me and said, *Do you remember the principle of the soft answer in Proverbs 15:1?*

I remembered, and I began to change my tune immediately. One man was standing up in the aisle, letting me have it with both barrels. "Excuse me," I said, "I need to ask your forgiveness. I made the assumption that you would want us to be a

225

part of your community without taking time to tell you what we intend to do. This is my fault, and I apologize for it. I promise you, we won't give out any food or clothing until you agree with what we're doing first."

As soon as I said that, the anger balloon popped and deflated all the tension. By the time the meeting was over, I was a hero. But the only thing that turned it around was the soft answer the Holy Spirit brought to my recollection. Time and time again, I've watched this principle work in my life. And if we're ever going to resolve our own conflicts, we have to learn to deflate anger in the same way.

My wife is a master at this. For instance, there are times when I have had every right (in my humble opinion) to be mad at her. I *wanted* to be mad because I had done the right thing and was deeply wronged for it. I'd been misunderstood, and it was time to get a little mad about it!

Then my wife would say, "Oh honey, I'm so sorry. I didn't know that I had done something that made you mad. Tell me what I can do to make it right."

How could I continue to be mad after a statement like that? I've even tried, but I just can't. Sometimes I would say, "Now, don't do that to me. I'm mad at you."

And she would say, "But I don't want you to be. What can I do?"

It's just like letting the air out of a balloon. It deflates all the anger inside. It's difficult to stay mad at somebody who is determined to be sweet like that and is giving a soft answer.

Practice controlling your tongue and giving a soft answer. Even when the atmosphere is charged with anger, follow the example given in the Bible and be slow to speak and quick to hear. It will help get the negotiation process going and start resolving conflicts.

There are four steps in the negotiation process that will take us from conflict to resolution. These are things that will make us successful negotiators no matter who we're dealing with. They are helpful whether we're buying a used car or resolving an interpersonal conflict with an old friend.

First of all, you and the other party must agree that the relationship has to be restored. This will be much easier to do if those involved are Christians who understand the Word.

The Bible makes it clear in numerous places that God wants us to be reconciled to our brother. If there is any ill will or ought, it should be taken care of immediately. Time and time again, we're told to be of one accord, of one mind, and of one heart. It is important to achieve this level of unity if we are going to experience the corporate anointing and power to change our community.

The body of Christ is not meant to be splintered. The Word of God says we're knit together in a bond of love. (Colossians 2:19) This leaves no room for schisms or divisions. Therefore, both parties in conflict must come into agreement that the conflict must be resolved before any further steps can be taken. And if we can't agree to that, there's no point in going any further.

Next, we need to let the other party know we're interested in coming to a mutually beneficial resolution. Assure them you're not out to impose your will or your point of view. Let them know that you have genuine concern for their welfare and that you're willing to yield to reason. The Bible calls it wisdom. Wisdom is peaceable, gentle, and easy to be entreated. (James 3:17)

Then, identify each party's perception as to the nature of the cause of the conflict. Find out what the battle is all about in the first place, why the schism occurred.

Secular studies have shown that somewhere between 50 and 75 percent of all interpersonal conflict is based on misunderstanding. So once you've gained an agreement that the conflict cannot be allowed to continue and you've let them know you have their best interests at heart, then you can begin identifying what the conflict is all about. Listen to each other's perception, even if it doesn't match your own. Let them tell you what they think the problem is all about, and wait until they finish before you begin formulating a response.

One way to let the other party know that you have truly heard them is to paraphrase what you heard them say after they've finished. Paraphrasing a party's explanation by stating it back to them is nothing more than repeating what you heard them say. When we know we have to repeat what they've said, we'll listen better. We'll become involved in their perspective of the argument, and we'll make sure we heard them right. Most importantly, *they'll* know we cared enough to listen and hear them clearly.

Jesus used the paraphrase as a matter of course with His disciples. A parable is a paraphrase of a principle from God's Word set in social terms that people can understand.

Once you've paraphrased their explanation of the problem, present your side as impersonally as possible. Don't start out saying something like, "Well, I think the problem is that you're just an insensitive turkey." That's not exactly an impersonal point of view!

Keep it from being accusatory or personal. Don't use blame, and remember you're working to solve the problem, not trying to add to it. Secular research indicates that over half of all interpersonal conflicts can be resolved at this level. Misunderstandings can be cleared up and conflict reduced when we simply tell the other party what we think.

However, if you've prayed, forgiven, and paraphrased and there still seems to be a genuine conflict of position, then you must go to the next step. And that is to clearly identify your refusal/compromise parameters. And by that, I mean you must decide exactly which points you are willing to give on and which points you can't. Clearly identify your bottom line, but be willing to give on any other point. Identify the point on which you cannot compromise, and come to an agreement on every other point.

As believers, our usual refusal parameters would tend to be anything that contradicts the Word of God. In other words, we can make compromises in other areas, but never where the Word of God is violated. Furthermore, we shouldn't compromise in those areas in which the Holy Spirit has spoken to us.

We should be able to compromise on any other point except those that go against what God has told us to do personally and what is found in His Word. Anything else we should probably be willing to give in on. And, usually, things that we refuse to compromise on which don't contradict these two points probably have something to do with ego or selfishness.

Think about it. Given what we have discovered about how poor relationship management tends to complicate our lives and rob us of God's light and presence, why would we want to let petty selfishness or pride keep us from resolving a conflict?

I've discovered through years in both business and ministry that many of the things I wanted to do that seemed to generate controversy weren't at the core of the problem in themselves. The problem I found was in the way I went about doing it. Controversy was generated because of the methods I used to pursue my plans.

It was my approach that was objectionable, not my goal.

However, when I changed my way of doing things to accommodate others, I was a success. I could avoid conflicts of interest without sacrificing my goals or objectives just by changing the way I approached and pursued my plans.

Resolving interpersonal conflicts is possible when we follow these four steps: prayer, forgiveness, paraphrase, and the setting of refusal/compromise parameters.

Once we believe the problem can be solved, God commands us to be reconciled to our brother or sister. So, it is possible to be reconciled; otherwise, He wouldn't have commanded it.

We may have to exercise our faith to initiate the process, but it can be resolved. We have to take God at His Word and believe the conflict is going to be resolved. Don't go into the process thinking that it's impossible to work out, because then it will be.

Believe the resolution will occur because God says it will if you follow these steps. Then, begin to agree with God that the conflict will be laid to rest. Also, let the person know you have an interest in coming to a mutually beneficial resolution. You might tell them that you're not trying to impose your will in the matter and that you have a genuine interest in their welfare. Take time to be sure you both understand what the conflict is all about, and, when you do, you may find the conflict resolved at this stage alone. Finally, come to an agreement and resolve the conflict.

Once a resolution has occurred and you've reached an agreement on the matter, you may need to draft some kind of documentation and accountability program to seal the agreement. Your need to use these things will depend on the depth of the division and how long it's been in effect. You may also need a pastor or some other third party as a witness to the mediation process. It may be helpful for someone else to hear the resolution you've come to. This provides a certain level of accountability that may be useful in the future.

Of course, you can't go drafting contracts with every relationship you form. I remember when our kids were living at home, I used to make up contracts all the time. I would get it written out and let them see it so they knew what our agreement was. "This is the deal," I would say. "This is what you've agreed to do, so don't come back to me in three months and say you didn't know."

That didn't always work, but it did provide a measure of accountability that, in many instances, was healthy and helpful.

However, in many relationships this approach won't work. There may be some people who never even get to step one, agreeing that there is a problem. He or she may be an unbeliever or somebody who's not a very mature Christian.

In fact, there may be some people with whom we simply cannot resolve conflict. The Bible tells us what to do in those cases. "Now I beseech you, brethren, mark them which cause divisions and offences contrary to the doctrine which ye have learned; and avoid them" (Romans 16:17). "Well," you may say, "that doesn't sound like walking in love to me." According to this passage, it's the best thing to do and it is walking in love. It is respecting the other person's choice not to resolve the conflict.

You see, there's a way to love this kind of person from a distance. For example, you can love him or her by praying without getting too close. That's still an act of giving in a very significant way but without getting involved in conflict.

You should not publicly single out anyone who won't resolve a conflict. That would be humiliating to them. God doesn't call us to humiliate anybody like that.

The meaning of the word *mark* means "to contemplate," to mentally take note of one who causes division.[2] Therefore, if we need to mark someone scripturally, we're mentally taking note of that person to avoid without publicly humiliating him or her.

The more contact you have with a contentious person, the more Satan is able to use that person to bring you pain. As long as that door is open to a relationship, the door is open to Satan. Avoid contentious people. Mark the person who doesn't want to settle a conflict with you, and stay clear of them until they are willing to resolve the conflict. In so doing, you avoid someone Satan wants to use to bring harassment into your life.

If somebody is determined to be divided and isolated from you by causing strife and contention, I would advise that you not try to minister to that person. He or she is living contrary to the Word, and that spirit of strife can try to infect you in order to separate you from the body of Christ.

Continue to love and pray for those people who are contentious and refuse to resolve conflicts with you for whatever reason. By praying for them, you are loving them, and love never fails. If you pray for them consistently, over time a door of opportunity will open for reconciliation to begin.

Once that door of opportunity is open, then you can begin to go through the process of resolving the problem.

After a relationship is healed, God has other means He can use to bring His purpose and provision to bear in our lives. By resolving an interpersonal conflict, we will have opened a door of influence to minister in somebody else's life for the better. We'll be managing that relationship properly and increasing the quality of our own life. The Word of God will produce good fruit, and life will get much simpler.

This is the way to lead a simplified life. True success in life only comes through following God's principles in His Word. True success is measured not only in dollars and cents, but also in terms of a healthy body, quality time spent with others, financial freedom, and, most of all, a vital relationship with Jesus Christ.

And yet the impartation of true success in life will occur only when we take the necessary steps to simplify our lives. According to God's Word, the entrance of His Word only brings light and understanding to the simple—not the half-witted, but rather the uncomplicated. (Psalms 119:130)

We've seen how to make our lives less complicated so that we're able to receive the life-changing truths and revelation God wants to give us. We know that, above all, our relationship with God is the most significant relationship we can ever have.

This is the way you simplify your life. God gives us one step to take at a time, and He allows us to grow into these truths. After all, that's what we're after. The whole reason we learn how to make things simpler is to spend more quality time with God and carry out His unique plan. Jesus is the Lover of our soul, and He's the one worth getting to know better.

ENDNOTES

Chapter 1

[1] Brown.

[2] Strong, "Hebrew," entry #7503, p. 110.

[3] Strong, "Hebrew," entry #6960, p. 102.

[4] Strong, "Hebrew," entry #3045, p. 3045.

Chapter 4

[1] Strong, "Hebrew," entry #3045, p. 3045.

Chapter 6

[1] Gray.

[2] Meystre.

[3] Bailey.

[4] Epstein.

Chapter 7

[1] Strong, "Greek," entry #3744, p. 53.

Chapter 8

[1] Strong, "Hebrew," entry #4643, p. 70, entry #6237, p. 92.

[2] Strong, "Greek," entry #2127, p. 33.

[3] Strong, "Greek," entry #4982, p. 70.

Chapter 9

[1] Strong, "Greek," entry #3784, p. 53.

Chapter 11

[1] Strong, "Greek," entry #26, p. 7.

Chapter 13

[1] Strong, "Greek," entry #4994, p. 70.

Chapter 14

[1] Strong, "Greek," entry #1246, p. 22.
[2] Strong, "Greek," entry #1849, p. 30.

Chapter 15

[1] Covey, p. 235.
[2] Vine, s.v. "skopeo," p.394.

REFERENCES

Bailey et al. "Measurements of relativistic time dilation for positive and negative muons in a circular orbit," *Nature* 268 (July 28, 1977) p. 301.

Brown, Francis, S.R. Driver, and Charles Briggs. *A Hebrew and English Lexicon of the Old Testament,* based on the lexicon of Wilhelm Gesenius. Boston: Houghton, Mifflin & Company, 1906.

Covey, Stephen R. *The 7 Habits of Highly Effective People.* New York: Simon & Schuster, 1989.

Epstein, Lewis Carroll. *Relativity Visualized.* San Francisco: Insight Press, 1987.

Gray, J.J. "Poincare, Einstein, and the theory of special relativity." *Mathematical Intelligencer* 17 (1995).

Meystre, Pierre and Marlan O. Scully, eds. "Proper Time Experiments in Gravitational Fields with Atomic Clocks, Aircraft, and Laser Light Pulses," *Quantum Optics, Experimental Gravity, and Measurement Theory,* Proceeding Conference, Bad Windsheim. New York: Plenum Press, 1981, 1983.

Strong, James. *Strong's Exhaustive Concordance of the Bible.* "Hebrew and Chaldee Dictionary," "Greek Dictionary of the New Testament." Nashville: Abingdon, 1890.

Vine, W.E. *Complete Expository Dictionary of Old and New Testament Words.* Nashville: Thomas Nelson, 1985.

PRAYER OF SALVATION

God in heaven, I come to You in the name of Your Son, Jesus. I confess that I haven't lived my life for You. I believe that Jesus is the Son of God. I believe that He died on the cross and rose again from the dead so I might have a better life now and eternal life in heaven. Jesus, come into my heart and be my Lord and Savior. From this day forward, I'll live my life for You to the best of my ability. In Jesus' name I pray, Amen.

If you have prayed this prayer to receive Jesus Christ as your Savior, or if this book has changed your life, we would like to hear from you.

ABOUT THE AUTHOR

 **Mac Hammond** is founder and senior pastor of Living Word Christian Center, a large and growing body of Christian believers in Brooklyn Park (a suburb of Minneapolis), Minnesota. He is nationally know as the host of the *Winner's Way* broadcast and is the author of several internationally distributed books. Mac is broadly acclaimed for his ability to apply the principles of the Bible to practical situations and the challenges of daily living.

Mac Hammond graduated from Virginia Military Institute in 1965 with a Bachelor's degree in English. Upon graduation, he entered the Air Force with a regular officer's commission and reported for pilot training at Moody Air Force Base in Georgia. He received his wings in November 1966, and subsequently served two tours of duty in Southeast Asia, accumulating 198 combat missions. He was honorably discharged in 1970 with the rank of Captain.

Between 1970 and 1980, Mac was involved in varying capacities in the general aviation industry including ownership of a successful air cargo business serving the Midwestern United States. A business merger brought the Hammonds to Minneapolis where they ultimately founded Living Word Christian Center in 1980 with 12 people in attendance.

After more than twenty years, that group of twelve people has grown into an active church body of more than 8,500 members. Today some of the outreaches that spring from Living Word include Maranatha Christian Academy, a fully-accredited, pre-K through 12th grade Christian school; Maranatha College, an evening college with an uncompromising Christian environment; Living Free Recovery Services, a state licensed outpatient treatment facility for chemical dependency; Club 3 Degrees, a cutting-edge Christian music club which is smoke/alcohol free; The Compassion Center, a multi-faceted outreach to inner- city residents; CFAITH, a cooperative online missionary outreach of hundreds of national and international organizations providing faith-based content and a nonprofit family oriented ISP; and a national and international media outreach which includes hundreds of audio/video teaching series, *A Call to Prayer* and the *Winner's Way* broadcasts, the *Prayer Notes* publication, and *Winner's Way* magazine.

OTHER BOOKS BY MAC HAMMOND

Angels at Your Service: Releasing the Power of Heaven's Host

Doorways to Deception: How Deception Comes, How It Destroys, and How You Can Avoid It

Heirs Together: Solving the Mystery of a Satisfying Marriage

The Last Millennium: A Revealing Look at the Remarkable Days Ahead and How You Can Live Them to the Fullest

Living Safely in a Dangerous World: Keys to Abiding in the Secret Place

Plugged In and Prospering: How to Find and Fill Your God-Ordained Place in the Local Church

Real Faith Never Fails: Detecting (and Correcting) Four Common Faith Mistakes

Yielded and Bold: Understanding the Unusual Move of God's Spirit

Positioned For Promotion: How to Increase Your Influence and Capacity to Lead

Winning in Your Finances: How to Walk God's Pathway to Prosperity

The Way of the Winner: Running the Race to Victory

Water, Wind & Fire: Understanding the New Birth and the Baptism of the Holy Spirit

Who God Is Not: Exploding the Myths About His Nature and His Ways

Winning the World: Becoming the Bold Soul Winner God Created You to Be

OTHER BOOKS BY LYNNE HAMMOND

The Master Is Calling: Discovering the Wonders of Spirit-Led Prayer

The Spiritual Enrichment Series *(four books by Lynne, recently retitled)*

> **When It's Time for a Miracle:** The Hour of Impossible Breakthroughs Is Now!
>
> **Staying Faith:** How to Stand Until the Answer Arrives
>
> **Heaven's Power for the Harvest:** Be Part of God's End-Time Spiritual Outpouring
>
> **Living in God's Presence:** Receive Joy, Peace, and Direction in the Secret Place of Prayer

Renewed in His Presence: Satisfying Your Hunger for God

When Healing Doesn't Come Easily

Secrets to Powerful Prayer: Discovering the Languages of the Heart

Dare to Be Free!

The Table of Blessing: Recipes From the Family and Friends of Living Word Christian Center

For more information about this ministry or a complete catalog of teaching tapes and other materials available, please write:

Mac Hammond Ministries

P.O. Box 29469

Minneapolis, MN 55429-2946

mac-hammond.org